# The Reluctant Landlord's GUIDE TO Profitable REAL ESTATE Property

## FINANCIAL AND MANAGEMENT FOUNDATIONS FOR MAKING LUCRATIVE REAL ESTATE INVESTMENTS

# Robert Pritchard

THE RELUCTANT LANDLORD'S GUIDE
TO PROFITABLE REAL ESTATE PROPERTY

Printed in the USA

ISBN (Print Edition): 978-0-9961482-0-7

ISBN (Kindle): 978-0-9961482-1-4

ISBN (eBook): 978-0-9961482-2-1

Library of Congress Control Number: 2015903655

Prepared for Publication By

Palm Tree Publications is a Division of Palm Tree Productions
www.palmtreeproductions.com

## LEGAL AND EARNINGS DISCLAIMER

To Contact the Author:

**www.pritchardconsultinginc.com**

# DEDICATION

For Ruth, the best wife,
mother and partner possible.

For Erin, Evan and Colleen.

# T R I B U T E

For inspiring aspirations of millions,
Dr. Thomas J. Stanley
1941-2015

Author of *The Millionaire Mind*

# ACKNOWLEDGEMENT

I initially assumed writing a book would be easy—a simple transfer of my thoughts onto paper with some semblance of purpose. I equated the process to the extraction of several tons of marble from the side of a quarry wall. Difficult? Yes, but with enough time, patience, and determination ... voilà! Done.

It is said that all Michelangelo really did was remove all the marble from his slab that didn't look like David. The statue had been in there the whole time and all he did was let it out for people to see. Uh huh.

My analysis thus is that getting my manuscript to my publisher was the equivalent of cutting the stone from the quarry wall. It did not start the transformation from pile of paper to book until arrival at Wendy K. Walters studio.

Wendy Walters is my chisel wielding artist and teacher. And she chiseled and hammered me with patience and determination until something that resembles what I now proudly call a book could be in your hands. Rest assured, without Wendy, all I would ever have otherwise had is an uncultured ream of dead tree.

Expert professionals make buying real estate easy, lucrative, and fun. Wendy Walters is the professional—the artist and expert behind this new "chapter" in my life. Thank you!

An investment in
knowledge pays
the best interest.

—Benjamin Franklin

# CONTENTS

## Part I—Foundations

## Part II—Mindset

## Part III—Business Acumen

# Part IV—Entrepreneurial Aspects

# List of Tables & Illustrations

# Part I

## F O U N D A T I O N S

The information contained in the following pages is representative of ideas only. It is in no manner intended to be used as plan for financial gain. This information is strictly for educational purposes. The rates, commissions, and returns are not in any way guaranteed.

Differing approaches will generate different returns. Because there are so many variables, these returns will rarely if ever be exactly the same for any two people. Use of this information is for a basis of understanding only. It is highly recommended that all individuals seek the assistance of the professionals necessary to establish their goals to achieve their financial desires.

CHAPTER ONE

# The Path Less Traveled

This book was designed for people who work for a living. It is for those who toil day to day—the backbone of society who make this country run—digging the ditches, stocking the shelves, putting out the fires, and teaching the children. It is written for blue collar workers without the privilege of vast assets derived from luck of birth as gilded offspring. It is also for white collar workers with enough foresight to recognize what constitutes an unstable work environment and want to be prepared. It is meant for students and small business owners trying to survive the inevitable potholes on the road to success. It is written for parents both alarmed and armed with enough foresight to hedge their bets for stability and growth in their economic microcosms. Most importantly, this book is dedicated to those who simply want more out of life, but never received any real financial education beyond how to balance a checkbook.

Today, the majority of the US population employed full-time works about 46 hours a week with 38% of those employed working over 50 hours. The average daily commute eliminates an additional 46 minutes from home life each day. Parent/teacher conferences, Little League, Boy Scouts (or Girl Scouts), and walking the dog all take an additional toll on available time. It would seem the weekends were made exclusively for mowing the lawn, washing the car, and handling household responsibilities. This is the routine we have come to accept. It is today's presumed path to the American Dream. There are problems though. It would seem that for every effort you put toward success, that effort is met with an equal and opposite force working against you. One such effort is advertising. Advertising is a huge machine designed to part you from those hard earned dollars. Everywhere you turn there are enticements designed by M.B.A.s and based upon studies by Ph.D.s to convince you that whatever it is they are selling, you need—print, radio, television, and internet—packaged and delivered repeatedly in smooth psychological sound bites. And, for those of you capable of ignoring the taunting efforts to partake from thee thy hard earned cash, there is the other problem—greed.

Almost daily we hear of horror stories. We cannot turn on the news without a report covering someone else who has worked all their lives only to find as they near retirement that their company is folding, their retirement accounts are subjected to the bankruptcy courts, and the future vitality of hundreds has been pilfered, victimized by boardroom vandals. Hundreds of thousands, millions in fact, were downsized due to negative economic times between 2008 and 2010 hugely impacting their lifestyles. ENRON was the biggest corporate failure ever … until GM.

Remember Circuit City? Washington Mutual? Blockbuster and Lehman Brothers? Survive that and manage to avoid even this tumultuous upheaval, actually make it through all the way to retirement seemingly unscathed, and now you have the Bernie Madoffs of the world to contend with. It seems each story is bigger and more alarming than the last. Yet, through it all, life still goes on. Even when we are victims ourselves, life goes on. In many cases life continues with the same practices, same attitudes, and same spending routines exactly as they had been before. This makes no sense. And yet, it makes perfect sense.

# WAIT, I HAD OPTIONS?

It all has to do with upbringing—repeated training from a very early age. Not until it's too late do people realize the path they've chosen is incorrect, unsuitable, or that there was even an optional path they might have taken. Who was there to teach them? Parents can only teach their children those things they themselves understand, intentionally and unintentionally. Convictions, prejudices, what matters and what does not matter to the parents is transferred to the children by how they act and all they say, often without conscious consideration as to how their children will interpret those actions. This is not premeditated, it is simply that many people do not see their children as impressionable in these regards, and therefore do not make the conscious effort to teach them things they do not understand. Rarely do parents encourage their children to consider other viewpoints apart from theirs and make up their own minds. The clearest way to illustrate this action is with religious affiliation.

Jewish parents teach Judaism to their children while children of Catholic parents are familiar with the sacrament of Confession and rosary beads. A Buddhist child will learn chants at an early age. An atheist will not take his children to any religious service—synagogue, mosque, church, or anything else.

It is unlikely that a child will develop an understanding of alternative beliefs beyond what they experience in the home unless there are strong outside influences. This is not usually a planned or concerted effort to ensure a child will only accept those beliefs of the parent; it is simply not a consideration at all. There are no sinister conspiracies at work here, just normal human behavior. You teach your children what you know. Indeed, how can you teach them what you yourself do not know?

My wife and I always maintained the notion we would introduce our children to as many things as we could to let them develop their own likes and dislikes. Though we wanted to guide them, it was important to us that they learn to make appropriate choices for themselves. This book is not about religion or philosophy; it is about personal finances and the theory behind personal wealth. But the imprinting of parental mindsets begin at a very early age and affects your views of work, money and wealth, so it must be addressed. Alternatives to their own current financial lifestyles are simply not recognized by the parents and as such cannot possibly be taught to the children. Just as there is no prerequisite to parenthood, the formal education processes in existence today do not teach financial savvy either. More than in any other area, children are left to their own devices in this regard.

If the parents have an understanding of the real intricacies of wealth building, are financially savvy themselves, and have the patience to actually teach their ways to their children, then these children will have an edge. There are many such fortunate folks out there. There are a great many more less fortunate without the benefit of such financial instruction. All that is left is the school of hard knocks—real life university. People have an overwhelming ability to recognize, with abject conviction, these terrible things happen all the time. But with that very same conviction, "know" (believe) nothing bad will ever happen to them!

# R I S K

There is no such thing as security, only varying degrees of risk. That is not a simple play on words, it is an absolute truth. Risk is a relative term and many people consider only one aspect of the word. Risk can be defined as the potential harm an action or event may cause—climbing Mount Everest is a risk. Five percent of those who have tried are entombed there. There is another type of risk as well, not patently as obvious as climbing Mount Everest. Inaction is risk. Inaction is failing to generate a future benefit by not carefully tending to an enterprise. The problem is that there is nothing to compare to. Fall off a mountain and you'll understand the risk instantly. How can you compare two results when you only live through one of them? To do this from a financial perspective, I recommend a solemn look around at your fellow neighbors. One may be standing in line at the food pantry while the other is taking a cruise every year with their grandkids. One believed his company and Social Security would adequately support him in retirement. Another never thought about retirement all. Still another did and collected an impressive library of reference, planned well, and took action accordingly.

**Inaction is risk. Inaction is failing to generate a future benefit by not carefully tending to an enterprise.**

My father-in-law worked for the railroad all his life. About four years before he was due to retire, the government took over in order to prevent the railroad from going into bankruptcy. In signing the deal the railroad gave my father-in-law, and thousands others, a *fait accompli*—allowing retirees a choice to receive either their railroad retirement or their Social Security, whichever was higher. They would not be permitted to collect both, which they had been promised and were expecting. In my father-in-law's case, expecting for over 30 years of service. It was a crushing blow for all involved.

We have been talking about the demise of Social Security for the past 30 years, ever since the treasury department raided the Social Security cookie jar and turned it into an IOU. In 2013 the federal government decided it needed money in advance of hitting the debt ceiling and so it considered raiding FERS (Federal Employees Retirement System). If this happens, the federal retirees had better take a good hard look at their futures as both their Social Security and their FERS will be reduced to IOU'S. Consider the number of federal employees today and we hand yet another very large problem to our kids.

Even those folks who make it all the way to retirement avoiding the entire gauntlet of doom and gloom—the Madoffs, the Enrons, the scams—and manage to retire with a comfortable 401k are often just ... lucky? The majority of people don't tend to the growth of their accounts with as much vigor as they do their window box vegetable gardens. They select securities from endless suggestions from vast hordes of "experts" gathered around the water cooler at the office. Here's a hint, your co-workers are probably listening to you more than you are to them. Instead of listening to people in the same boat you are in, why not try the advice of true experts? The library and the internet are great places to start. There are literally thousands of books on the subject. Start with the best sellers list, they are probably best sellers for good reason. A partial list of recommended reading material is in the appendix at the back of this book. I suggest prolific reading and absorption, and that you start today.

Failing to plan has the same result as planning to fail. This is not a secret so why do so many of us ignore it? Why do so many of us believe (or rather "know") that the stories in the news will never happen to us? We tell ourselves lies. "The other company will fail, not mine ... my investments are safe ... I know my advisor." There is no secret hidden obscure power like gravity enveloping us and protecting us from financial ruin. There is no fairy tale force directing our lives down some yellow brick road of gullibility. No, it is much more mundane than that. I am referring to our training where we spend the first 18 to 25 years getting ready for employment, preparing to lend our talents to the goods and services industries, and becoming assets to society at large, but not necessarily assets to ourselves. At no time during the basic education cycle do we learn the necessary arts involved in becoming independent thinkers—that often happens only by chance. We have to take control. Nobody is going to be responsible for our future but us.

The real problem is that we don't know we are actually missing anything. How could we know we are not doing something if even those instructing us don't know it either? I have had people work for me that had no idea how to balance a checkbook or what purpose such action even had. Are these people stupid? No. They simply never saw a checkbook in their lives. How many times have you gone to the checkout counter at a store and waited patiently for the cashier to figure out how much change to give you? Have you had one need a calculator to it figure out? Stores now have automatic "changers" that spits out the coins for the cashier and "self serve" lines eliminate the human element completely. With the convenience of debit and credit cards and the use of online and mobile banking, an entire generation will likely never sit down to reconcile where their money went, let alone why.

They say it takes money to make money. I disagree. It helps for sure, but knowledge will get you a lot further. Since you made the conscious effort to read this far, you have a head start. For those souls who have a firm understanding, there are specialty schools that focus on entrepreneurial skills (such as Wharton School of Finance) but more often than not, people (Donald Trump excluded) go to school to become useful to society in a trade or profession. They only end up as entrepreneurs by default. Often one has to get seriously upset with the grind of the job (read *Home Made,* the story of Home Depot) or the audacities of the corporate world (Scott Adams, *Dilbert* cartoonist) before welling up the overpowering and all-consuming need to venture out and become independent

There are thousands upon thousands of impressive biographies and financial instructional guides. One of my favorites is suggested as parables from esoteric clay tablets and translated for millennia currently carrying the modern title of *The Richest Man in Babylon*, a great short story and entirely believable as being written thousands of years ago. I recommend reading biographies of as many successful people as you can find—stories of men like Sam Walton, Akita Morito, Henry Ford, John D. Rockefeller, Trump and, my personal favorite, Paul Reichmann (for the good and the bad). Now, that is a short list of highly motivated and impressively accomplished people, and it is a list I do not pretend be a part. So who am I to sit here and tell you how you can be like them?

My own story is considerably more modest, and as such I suspect easier for the audience I am trying to reach to relate to. Simply put, I have more in common with the typical reader. I worked 40 hours a week at a regular job like most of my blue collar peers. It was not a bad job; it paid the bills and afforded me a modest home and an annual vacation. We dine out more often than we should and both my wife and I were Boy Scout and Girl Scout leaders. Life is good. However, I also have two older children who both attend a private university, both have taken multiple trips to Europe and Asia as rewards—incentives we placed on good school work. My salary would not pay for these. We have five vehicles, all paid for. My job would not cover the cost of these either. We have no mortgage on our house, twelve acres of land we play on, and we subsidized my mother's living expenses. Again, my salary would not cover these expenses.

I quit high school in the tenth grade, endured the typical rough ride offered a high school dropout, and completed my high school education only after joining the Air Force, not entirely of my own free choice. Once I completed my four year tour of duty I returned home and attended college in pursuit of a career in architecture. I always had an artistic talent and designing buildings was a great release. I graduated with an associate's degree in building technology and went to work for my architecture professor in his one-man office. I did everything there was to do until his untimely death a year and a half later when an undiagnosed aortic aneurism took his life while sitting at his kitchen table grading papers. He was 53. His wife lost the house and his son was forced to quit college. This was a wake-up call for me. It is worth repeating, there is no such thing as security.

I enrolled in a co-op architectural school, requiring classroom attendance as well as working forty hours per week in the field. With my previous experience I was able to secure another position in a one-man office and it went well, but I found it boring and I never finished school. I soon found I hated working in an office environment. I enjoyed designing, but the clients would come in and change everything we designed because of cost considerations. In my naivety I would argue. After all it was our design … so what if it was their money! We knew what was best for the client, but in the end they (and their money) always won. To me, young and naïve, it was all quite frustrating. Later I would realize the people who hired architects always seemed to have more money than the architects they hired. Hmmm.

One moment of realization came while sitting in my office entertaining a client. The boss was late getting back from a job site. In a small office you designed the buildings, answered the phone, made the coffee, and in this case, entertained the clients as well. This particular client was a developer who had a defunct golf course and was having us design a warehouse for one of his clients. He and I got to talking.

I suggested he looked young and asked how he got off to such a good start that he could afford to buy a golf course at his age. He laughed and told me, "I didn't have a pot to piss in, let alone money to buy a golf course!" Now this piqued my curiosity more than just a little bit and I ran several thousand thoughts through my mind. First and foremost, if he didn't have "a pot to piss in," how and why was he having us design an 80,000 square foot office and warehouse for him? More to the point, how was he paying for it? So I asked and he readily explained. What he told me permanently changed my line of thinking. He did not own the golf course, but rather he had used his own life's savings and borrowed the necessary funds from family and friends to secure an "option" on a golf course for five years. He would have the right to develop it as a viable industrial site, and would consequently secure financing for the purchase based upon the rents paid by the corporate clients. Profits would be shared with the site contractor he lined up to put in the roads and utilities. He had spent everything he had and/or was able to secure in gaining approvals and site development for three initial pad sites. He hoped to get those buildings complete and rented within the first three years. As of our meeting, the first two were up and occupied and we were working on the third.

During that meeting he recommended I read a couple of books. If I was seriously interested in what he'd had to say I would show it by finding them and reading them, after which we would talk again. Five months later I owned a three family house. I still have that house and I still have those books. I still worked 40 hours a week, but no longer in architecture. As you will see, until retirement, I fixed airplanes for the Air National Guard.

CHAPTER TWO

# Goals

What do you want to accomplish financially? Did you buy this book for yourself or was it a gift? Did you buy it for someone else as a gift, but then decide to read it first? If you initiated it great, you have a head start. I don't have to try to convince you there are other ways to protect yourself financially, you already know it or you wouldn't have wasted your money or time on this book in the first place. But before we get into all that, let me finish my brief story.

I was married at age 25, only a year before my encounter with the developer I spoke of in the last chapter. I quit school in Boston and returned to New York, took a job with yet another small architectural firm, and began looking earnestly at potential investments. Within a couple of years my wife and I had purchased and/or built a few homes, including the purchase of a four family income property in a partnership with my new boss, which turned out to be a highly a successful long-term endeavor. Shortly after this I made an expensive mistake. I allowed myself to be talked into another partnership with one of the other employees who, after seeing the success the boss and I were enjoying, just had to get involved as well. However, his ideas did not reflect mine. My operational style did not mirror his and we clashed on every level. Post mortem analysis would show I allowed myself to stray too far from what I understood and blindly rode a wave of success—with an "S" on my chest and a cape of invincibility. It was a miserable time and I lost several tens of thousands of dollars chasing desires that did not belong to me. Through it all my boss and I maintained our partnership and ultimately remained in business together for 21 years. This second partnership took three years to dissolve and ended about the same time my wife and I were expecting our first child.

I believe there is a huge difference between having a family and raising a family. I vowed to spend the time with my kids which I did not enjoy with my parents while growing up, so I scaled back and settled down. Up to this time I had fallen into a routine of putting in between 60 and 90 hours a week—working in the office by day and renovating property by night and on weekends. The world of architecture is sporadic at best which I gave up in exchange for a nice "secure" civilian position with the New York Air National Guard as a full-time aircraft mechanic. I quickly rekindled my military training and settled down with the intent to raise a family. I was now 30 years old. Though I still maintained and managed property, it was to a considerably lesser extent.

> There is a huge difference between having a family and raising a family.

Five months into this new position my life focused on our daughter. When she was born what remained was a three family income property, a two family income property, a single family rental property, and a three acre parcel intended for the construction of our "dream" home. I was also the managing partner in the four family income property. All other properties were subsequently sold.

We had pared down considerably and slipped comfortably into a routine when I made our second costly mistake.

We abandoned the notion of building a dream home for ourselves when an opportunity came along to rebuild and purchase the home belonging to my wife's parents. Unfortunately, this came with conditions we both knew, but collectively refused to acknowledge. We commenced headlong into a massive hundred thousand dollar, gut-wrenching renovation on a house we would not own until after renovations were complete at our expense. In addition, we would have to refinance the property in our names after obtaining a new certificate of occupancy. The issue we refused to deal with was the stipulation that once the project was complete, the in-laws would live there as well. We would be required to share the house and the living space within. We sold the acreage, poured heart and soul into this blindingly exciting new project and in the end, could not live in the house under the arrangements we agreed to. Ultimately, we sold the house. By the time we realized our foolishness and came to grips with the only remaining solution, the real estate market turned south. Once the house did finally sell, the amount was barely enough to cover the agreed upon purchase price which the in-laws received. None of the expensive renovation was recovered. By the time of the sale of that house, our first child was four and our second was two. But my wife was away from her family and we were happily married once again.

With this last major mistake behind us we moved into the single family home we had been renting and concentrated fully on raising a family. This was also the first time we sat back and analyzed where we were, and more importantly, where we wanted to go over the course our lives. In a sense, everything from the beginning to this point had simply happened. From here on out it was more or less haphazardly "planned."

# W H A T   I S   " W E A L T H Y " ?

When forced to answer an open-ended question such as, "Where you want to go in life?" it can be quite difficult to know where to begin. How do you start to address something you cannot understand? It's not like, "I am here, I want to be there." Think of it as light and dark, easy enough, right? Not to someone who cannot see both. A blind person cannot fully comprehend light without ever having had the opportunity to compare it to darkness. Likewise, an individual seeking wealth cannot truly understand all that is entailed in the manifestation of such achievement until he has attained it himself and can honestly compare the differences. So, "Where am I now and where do I want to go?" remains an open-ended question.

Test this synopsis by asking several friends and co-workers what it is to be wealthy, or where they want to go financially with their lives. You might hear one utter the popular yet anti-climatic cliché, "To be independently wealthy." Ask ten people for their definition of the term "wealthy" and you will get ten different answers every time. Dictionaries define wealthy in three ways: having great wealth, characterized by or suggestive of wealth, and rich in character. For most people it equates to a physical object (such as a boat, or a plane, or a private island in the South Pacific) or an arbitrary goal (such as having a bigger house or owning my own business). But it is actually none of these definitions or any of the personal suggestions above. Wealth is all of the above realized in a setting unique to you, only not manifested in objects, but rather in capability. Henry Ford was asked, "What would you do if I took away all your worldly possessions?" Without hesitation he retorted, "Go ahead, I'll have them all back in three years." Would you?

Is a person with a 112 foot yacht with matching helicopter on the back wealthy? If they are the CEO of a corporation perhaps, but if that corporation is ENRON does this change your perspective? What if the people landing in their private jet while you wait to depart from your economy class seat are only there because they won a lottery last year? Your perception may not (and often does not) match with the reality of a little deeper look. There are an awful lot of used yachts and private jets in the repo lots today.

Let's get back to the term "independently wealthy" for a moment. There are a lot of people on the paid channels pushing their "Become Independently Wealthy" regimens while standing in front of large expensive homes with huge pools and decks, surrounded by scantily clad women. Maybe they are their own homes, more likely, they are not. I'm not here to judge, but let me suggest that a little creative marketing on Madison Avenue's part goes a long way towards selling books and packing lecture halls. Whether the mansion in the background is their own or not is not important, convincing you to buy their programs is. There have been many of those schemes over the millennium and they all work to some degree. That is to say, every book and seminar you take in—whether you spend pennies or thousands of dollars—will gain you some degree of added benefit and add to your knowledge base. What doesn't work is the fulfillment of your expectations of instant gratification after making the purchase.

It is not (usually) the data in this material that is flawed, rather it is the mindset of the reader where the problem lies. You, as the reader, cannot under any circumstances turn on a proverbial light switch in your mind and move away from the long practiced routine you have established and lived by. You will not become an independent thinker after reading one book or attending one seminar. It is not easy. It takes time and it takes a lot of practice. You cannot become rich overnight in any endeavor with anything other than luck—and luck per-say does not exist—only the perception of luck. The perception of having luck in the lottery can only come if you buy a ticket. How many tickets do you have to buy to stack the odds in your favor? If you had enough money to buy one of every possible combination you would run out of time buying them long before the lottery went off, and it still wouldn't be one of your tickets that won. Wealthy people purchase very few lottery tickets. With a multitude of media programs available today, you can stack the odds in your favor not by buying the books and tapes and sitting in the lecture halls but by reading, learning, and practicing all you can with them once you absorb the material. Although many authors will suggest otherwise, what they offer you are not get-rich quick schemes. They are polished (and often much embellished) blueprints. The authors (with some help from others) carefully perfected their programs through much trial and error to scratch and climb above the hordes. Their systems are merely tools. Like a car, whether a fine imported sports car or an old clunker that barely runs, a car is a tool that will serve but one purpose: to get you from where you are … to where you want to go. In the end, it's up to you to turn the key, choose a destination, and drive. Status symbols not included.

Further, these programs are available in your local library. Let someone else spend the hundreds of dollars they typically cost. You do not need to spend a dime on any of them. On that same note there are books I have that I reference time and again. I recommend these be in every personal library. I put reading lists in the appendix based on where you are financially at the time you read this book. I recommend you build your own library and that you start soon. In some cases it took folks fifty years to develop the habits they have today. Starting is the hard part, but you are reading this, which means you are at least curious. Which brings us back to our original question, "Where do you want to go?"

# DETERMINATION

My wife and I decided we wanted to join the ranks of the "independently wealthy." At the time we had no idea where that was, what it looked like, or how to get there. Looking back, if we would even have been able to recognize it if we did get there. So we set out to do something without any clue about what might be entailed. We had but one thing: determination. Determination should not be confused with ambition. There are a lot of ambitious people who would like to be CEO, but with no determination to do anything to get themselves there. Determination is something that can be grasped; it can be shaped, and molded. More importantly, it can be broken down into laymen's terms—to a single word: goals. Determination can become goals. Goals can become plans, and plans are executable. Set yourself a goal.

One of my early goals was to retire on a 66' open back Choy-Lee Motor Yacht. Why?

Because I saw a picture of it, and I liked it.

*Shown is a modern 68' version.*
*The original photo was lost ... but you get the idea!*

I had that picture hanging over my desk for years. Half a dozen years later we bought a brand new 24-1/2' cabin cruiser with a galley and an aft cabin as a starter—only to find out my wife didn't handle the motions all that swell—pun most certainly intended! So we traded in our plan for the Choy-Lee Motor Yacht for five-star world travel plans, and we traded in the cruiser for twelve acres of land.

It's okay to change the plan. But you have to have a plan to change.

I took this time to tell you where I've been. Read the book, *The Master Builders* (the story of Paul Reichmann and his company Olympia and York) to see how far a person can go.

As far as goals are concerned, many folks have a New Year's resolution to lose weight. At 210 pounds on New Year's Eve, setting the goal to get down to 180 by next year is great, but few accomplish this feat because of the way the goal is designed. Setting a goal to lose 30 pounds in a year is a daunting task and very difficult. It is about the same as saying, "I want to be a millionaire by the time I'm 50." The problem is how to achieve the goal. How do you get there? The number is too big to see and the end is never within sight. Well, at least it doesn't come into focus until the twilight of December, about the same time you realize you gained five pounds for the year. You had probably forgotten all about the initial goal by the end of January anyway. Setting a series of goals to lose two and half pounds each month for a year is achievable. It can go on each page of the calendar as a subtle reminder and with twelve reminders throughout the year the odds are you won't completely forget the process that made the goal important to you when you initially made it. Setting financial goals to establish saving, eliminate credit card debt and a car payment is no different. Learn to walk before entering a marathon.

I've had an interesting time trying to figure out where I was going financially in life and over the years I have found one common denominator. Very few people outside the professional money management world understand much of how the immensely intricate and versatile worlds of finance really work. In fact there are relatively few who have any understanding of anything but the most basic functions of financial markets. I know this because I have asked an awful lot of people for advice over the years, and in almost every case they did not know any more than I did. I began to ponder why this might be. What I found was a profoundly simple answer: nobody ever taught them anything. Or, they were taught only the limited knowledge of their teachers, parents, and employers—collectively, not amounting to much. The exception is perhaps those pupils of the school of hard knocks, but even then, that applies only to those that actually paid attention to the material presented. (I attended that school twice before learning to adhere to the lessons.)

For many, how to balance a checkbook and being told, "credit card balances are bad" is about it. Banks earn millions every year on returned check and overdraft protection fees, which pretty much indicates a lack of attention during that lesson. And, as the incredibly profitable credit industry indicates, most missed the credit card class as well. But even those whose upbringing did manage to convey the points of "frugality is good" and "debt is bad" are not astute to the world of financial savvy. We are all taught to "save for a rainy day." But to be able to spend that savings during rainy days is not the most accurate reason for saving it in the first place. Many of us have heard the lesson of the power behind compound interest and how remarkably fast reinvested interest can grow account balances. If there is a catastrophic calamity that requires use of these funds, great, you have saved for that purpose. But recent trends increasingly suggest these rainy days are in the form of income reduction from job loss. Therefore, a much more compelling reason to save is to have that savings generate an income for you during a rainy period.

Investments of all kinds should generate income. Bank savings accounts will guarantee your money safe and pay ¼ of 1% if you deposit it with them. High yield bonds may pay 6% but there are no guarantees your initial deposit will be safe should you need it. Therefore we should be balancing risk against rate, find that comfortable point in the middle, and settle back for the long haul in case that rainy day catches up to us. No matter what you save for or why, you still need to keep an eye on the results.

# THE RIGHT QUESTIONS

Done correctly it is easy to figure out your goals. If you want to have $20,000 a year in income available should you need it, and you are receiving 4% on your investment choice, you need to have $500,000 invested. ($20,000 / .04 = $500,000) At 5%, you need $400,000 invested. ($20,000/.05 = $400,000)

I'm betting that if you are reading this, you don't have that kind of cash sitting around.

A friend we'll call Steve had a part time lawn mowing business. Steve was a very frugal individual and set up a bank savings account into which he dumped some of his excess earnings. At the time I spoke with him he had amassed a balance in this savings account of $25,000. But over the four years or so, only a few of the dollars in the account was earned through interest, he had worked hard to earn it all. Not bad for a part time endeavor by a guy who works forty hours a week and has an hour and forty minute commute—each way, but it was a lot less than it could have or should have been. He asked me what he should do with the money in the account which was collecting only a quarter of a percent interest from the bank. Most of us would love to have that problem!

This book is not about answering these kinds of questions in any direct fashion. It is simply about recognizing the need to ask those kinds of questions in the first place. It is about the financial education we never received. I asked Steve, as I am asking you, to look at it a little differently. If he earned a 4% return on that money by buying a bond, how many lawns would he have to cut to earn the same $1,000 that bond would pay in interest? It was a lot. We talked about the upkeep of the equipment, how many hours he spent on the business and so on. I asked him to tell me why he worked so hard to generate the dollars he saved, but was not tending to the "cash flow" machine that was sitting in his bank account essentially idle. With the right finesse the leftover funds in that account would be producing just as much or more than he could earn in actually cutting those lawns.

The light switched on. He was ready to do something about it. I lent him my Ric Edleman books and sent him home to do some homework—homework that wouldn't take much more time than he would have spent mowing a couple more lawns. I did not tell him the answer he was looking for, but I did plant the idea that there is a lot more than the limited knowledge he possesses available if he knows where to look. The good news is he recognized enough to understand he was not as astute as he could be.

Not all the alleged "experts" are actually experts either.

About 1984, shortly after returning to New York from Boston, my wife and I had a meeting with business consultant/financial planner of whom we asked a similar "What to do?" question. We told him we wanted to be millionaires by the time we were fifty. After telling him we had nothing to invest and that we wanted to become millionaires, he chuckled and said, "Me too." Then he proceeded to laugh us out of the office. I've never seen him since and I don't know if he ever learned what we learned, but it would be interesting to compare our histories today.

Since that date with the financial planner I have done a lot of research, read a lot of books, and attended a few seminars on a variety of subjects. In short I have undergone a complete psychological reprogramming about the way I think about money, what money is, and how it is accumulated. Unless it is explained early, reinforced daily, practiced, exploited, and expanded continuously you are as I was, behind the curve, but you are not out of the game. Start by reading. Practice what you read. Study people you'd like to emulate and put into practice what you learn. Through it all I suggest one last little tidbit, never forget where you came from. You'll need that deeply embellished before you can appreciate where it is you get to once you arrive.

# CREATE MOMENTUM

The pursuit of wealth should not limit your studies to attending financial seminars and reading financial books. Become well read on multiple subjects. Teach yourself to be prolific at absorbing nonfiction material of all sorts. I read many biographies of successful people, books on negotiation, goals, project management, sales techniques, public speaking, how-to this and that, and self-improvement material of all kinds. None of this goes to waste and from all can be garnered a morsel of intellectual nourishment. Set goals to read a book a month, save a thousand dollars in six months, to eliminate a car payment, limit television to two hours and walk a mile a day … and get rid of your credit card debt!

Working on six or seven things at the same time is not as hard as it may seem. Your goals will begin to take on a life of their own and you'll quickly see how they all tend to feed upon each other, especially once you begin to achieve a few. Minor successes translate themselves into a feeling of euphoria. Like a base hit in a little league game transforms the crowd. Keep the momentum alive with goals. This is the notion behind the aura of the "lucky" person. This is how the perception of luck is transposed. It is not luck at all. It is knowledge and the constant expansion of understanding.

If you don't have the time or inclination to research the means yourself, there are a few folks willing to help you with your goals and we'll take a look into that tank in the next chapter.

CHAPTER THREE

# Investment Comparisons

There exists today a multi-trillion dollar industry with sound basis in questionable claims. That industry is the investment industry. I call it the shark tank (not to be confused with the popular TV show). Understand this very clearly: no one on the face of this planet will ever assume responsibility for what another person chooses to regard as fact or fiction. The industry built for your investment needs is primarily a commission based industry. Whatever you buy as an investment will generate a commission to the person from whom you make the purchase. Without batting an eye, there should be little doubt as to which of the two of you has the other person's best interest at heart. We will delve considerably deeper into this, but first we need to understand a few of the facts regarding some of the so-called investment strategies that exist and what these strategies are really all about. The easiest way to do that is to reduce all strategies to equal terms to ensure we compare apples to apples.

Let's begin with a brief overview of typical investment categories and the forces behind them. This is important as it will lay the foundation for further understanding. I intend to upset everyone here, so if I leave someone out I apologize in advance!

# MONEY DOUBLING

To keep this simple we will touch on five categories for a $50,000 investment to see how long it would take to double your money in that investment based on historical returns. In addition we will look at what each investment category would have generated over a five year period. We'll look at the short term and long term issues of cash, bonds, stocks, precious metals, and income producing real estate. I will also provide a recommended list of references at the end for you to learn more and achieve even greater understanding.

- **Cash:** will be considered a box of hundreds, a savings or a checking account, or any sort of money market account.

- **Bonds:** includes bank CDs, US Government savings bonds, corporate, municipal and junk bonds.

- **Stock:** comprises individual shares of a company, mutual funds, and exchange traded funds (ETF).

- **Precious Metals:** are bullion itself in any form, coins, bars, or ingots. When we talk about coins, understand this does not include collector coins from the 1800s—these have much higher values than just their metal content and would confuse the category. We are discussing mint issue bullion coins, bars or ingots, but not traded shares of metals commodities.

- **Income Producing Real Estate:** will be any non-owner occupied premises, residential or commercial, individually owned or owned in partnership, but not included in any form of publically traded Real Estate Investment Trust (REIT). This does not include vacant land for speculative purposes.

I don't pretend this is all there is to choose from. There are millions of choices, hybrids, derivatives, and gimmicks in each of the categories above. All have been reduced to one of the aforementioned groups for sake of simplification. What we are looking at is the vehicle only: the methods for obtaining the investment vehicle, and the return on the choice made for comparison and using average rates of return for about the past 90 years. In addition, there are things that affect one category that do not affect another; commissions, taxes, use of borrowed funds and governmental incentives. We will take multiple views of these categories where these factors apply, adding each impacting factor separately in an effort of legitimate comparison.

# CASH

Where cash is concerned there is no cost in obtaining the investment. That is to say, there is no fee for purchasing the investment vehicle (cash), whether that means in a box under the bed, or in a money market account at the local savings and loan. The return at today's rate is miniscule and will probably not break one percent. If we assume it to be one full percent for the example it would take about 72 years to double your money. This is known as the "Rule of 72." Any interest rate when divided into 72 will give the number of years required to double the investment being made. If the interest rate is, as in this case, 1% then it will take 72 years to double your money: 72/1 = 72 years.

If the interest rate is 3.9% then: 72 /3.9 = 18.5 years.

Likewise, if you know you want to double your money in say five years, you can use this rule to help you determine the rate of return you will need to reach your goal.

**72 / 5 years = 14.4%**

This calculation shows you will need an investment generating 14.4% annual interest. Good luck. Our cash investment is safe (unless it is under the bed) and it will not disappear in loss of principal due to your making a bad investment. Inflation not included. Historically (since 1913), the average interest rate has been 3.9%. Using this, your original investment of $50,000 would take 18 years to become $100,000. At the end of our five year experiment, you would have $60,540.74 in your account ... assuming you could find a 3.9% rate of return today. This does not apply to the box under your bed.

## *Cash I*

| Year | Beginning Balance | Interest 3.9% | Interest Earned | Ending Balance | |
|---|---|---|---|---|---|
| 1 | $ 50,000.00 | $ 0.04 | $ 1,950.00 | $ 51,950.00 | |
| 2 | $ 51,950.00 | $ 0.04 | $ 2,026.05 | $ 53,976.05 | |
| 3 | $ 53,976.05 | $ 0.04 | $ 2,105.07 | $ 56,081.12 | |
| 4 | $ 56,081.12 | $ 0.04 | $ 2,187.16 | $ 58,268.28 | |
| 5 | $ 58,268.28 | $ 0.04 | $ 2,272.46 | $ 60,540.74 | After 5 years |
| 6 | $ 60,540.74 | $ 0.04 | $ 2,361.09 | $ 62,901.83 | |
| 7 | $ 62,901.83 | $ 0.04 | $ 2,453.17 | $ 65,355.00 | |
| 8 | $ 65,355.00 | $ 0.04 | $ 2,548.85 | $ 67,903.85 | |
| 9 | $ 67,903.85 | $ 0.04 | $ 2,648.25 | $ 70,552.10 | |
| 10 | $ 70,552.10 | $ 0.04 | $ 2,751.53 | $ 73,303.63 | |
| 11 | $ 73,303.63 | $ 0.04 | $ 2,858.84 | $ 76,162.47 | |
| 12 | $ 76,162.47 | $ 0.04 | $ 2,970.34 | $ 79,132.81 | |
| 13 | $ 79,132.81 | $ 0.04 | $ 3,086.18 | $ 82,218.99 | |
| 14 | $ 82,218.99 | $ 0.04 | $ 3,206.54 | $ 85,425.53 | |
| 15 | $ 85,425.53 | $ 0.04 | $ 3,331.60 | $ 88,757.12 | |
| 16 | $ 88,757.12 | $ 0.04 | $ 3,461.53 | $ 92,218.65 | |
| 17 | $ 92,218.65 | $ 0.04 | $ 3,596.53 | $ 95,815.18 | |
| 18 | $ 95,815.18 | $ 0.04 | $ 3,736.79 | $ 99,551.97 | |
| 19 | $ 99,551.97 | $ 0.04 | $ 3,882.53 | $ 103,434.50 | Doubled |

Using the rule of 72 @ 3.9% it will take 18.5 years to double

Table 3.1—Cash I

# B O N D S

Bonds are loans. A government bond is literally an I.O.U. to the United States Treasury department given to you when you lend the government money. They are the safest security you can purchase, but with that low risk come lower returns. Municipal bonds are issued by local governments, corporate bonds by corporations.

Buying certain government bonds are free of fees. Other kinds of bonds will have various fees associated with their purchase. Bonds have either a fixed interest rate or a fixed purchase price that will mature to the predetermined value upon completion of the holding period. Since the rates are fixed, the time required to double your money in bonds varies greatly and is wholly dependent upon the particular bonds interest rate. However, EE Series government bonds peaked at 7% and at that rate would have doubled in a little more than 10 years. With current interest rates, it would take more than 58 years to double your investment.

Municipal bonds, corporate bonds, and junk bonds (high yield, high risk corporate loans made to companies with bad credit, takeover candidates and other risky situations) all have different rates, some have tax advantages and so on. Bond rates are both partial and reciprocal to the security of the initial investment. The higher the rate sought, the higher the risk you place on your investment. We will figure a 5% return on our bonds for argument's sake however, there are higher rates available and, of course, there are lower rates as well. No matter the rate of return there are fees associated with the purchase of most bonds and these fees vary with the type of bond and amount purchased.

For our example we will agree to a $5.00 fee charged per $1,000 in bonds. Therefore, for our purchase of $50,000 in bonds, a fee of $250.00 is charged on both ends for handling the transaction—once for buying, once for selling. Even so, you would double your investment in just over 14 years. At the end of our five year model you would have $63,479.89.

### *Bonds I*

| Year | Beginning Balance | Commission Paid | Interest 5% | Interest Earned | Ending Balance | |
|---|---|---|---|---|---|---|
| | $ 50,000.00 | $ 250.00 | | | $ 49,750.00 | |
| 1 | $ 49,750.00 | | $ 0.05 | $ 2,487.50 | $ 52,487.50 | |
| 2 | $ 52,487.50 | | $ 0.05 | $ 2,624.38 | $ 55,111.88 | |
| 3 | $ 55,111.88 | | $ 0.05 | $ 2,755.59 | $ 57,867.47 | |
| 4 | $ 57,867.47 | | $ 0.05 | $ 2,893.37 | $ 60,760.84 | |
| 5 | $ 60,760.84 | | $ 0.05 | $ 3,038.04 | $ 63,798.88 | |
| | $ 63,798.88 | $ 318.99 | | | $ 63,479.89 | After 5 years |
| 6 | $ 63,798.88 | | $ 0.05 | $ 3,189.94 | $ 66,988.83 | |
| 7 | $ 66,988.83 | | $ 0.05 | $ 3,349.44 | $ 70,338.27 | |
| 8 | $ 70,338.27 | | $ 0.05 | $ 3,516.91 | $ 73,855.18 | |
| 9 | $ 73,855.18 | | $ 0.05 | $ 3,692.76 | $ 77,547.94 | |
| 10 | $ 77,547.94 | | $ 0.05 | $ 3,877.40 | $ 81,425.34 | |
| 11 | $ 81,425.34 | | $ 0.05 | $ 4,071.27 | $ 85,496.61 | |
| 12 | $ 85,496.61 | | $ 0.05 | $ 4,274.83 | $ 89,771.44 | |
| 13 | $ 89,771.44 | | $ 0.05 | $ 4,488.57 | $ 94,260.01 | |
| 14 | $ 94,260.01 | | $ 0.05 | $ 4,713.00 | $ 98,973.01 | |
| 15 | $ 98,973.01 | | $ 0.05 | $ 4,948.65 | $ 103,921.66 | |
| | $ 103,921.66 | $ 519.61 | | | $ 103,402.05 | Doubled |

Table 3.2—Bonds I

# S T O C K S

Stock is ownership in a corporation. When you own stock in a corporation you own a tiny percentage of that corporation along with its assets and earnings. Unlike bonds you cannot purchase U.S. Government stock. This is because while it is possible to lend money to the government, it is not possible to purchase a piece of it … politicians notwithstanding. Mutual funds and exchange traded funds (ETFs) are comprised of a pool of money gathered from many investors and operated by fund managers. Their "job" is to invest the fund's capital in attempt to increase value for the fund's investors. Stocks, mutual funds, exchange traded funds, and all the instruments in between have a fee associated with their purchase. In order to be safely invested in stock, requires a portfolio of different stocks, or funds, to ensure diversification. For a portfolio of $50,000 in stock funds, assume $250 worth of fees or commissions. Like bonds, you will pay this fee both when you purchase and again when you sell. It is the price of doing business. The average return on the stock market in general since 1913 has been about 8% depending on what source you use for researching these things. I chose this as a nice round number for our experiment. Let's assume you reinvest dividends and do not engage in selling and buying the stock after your initial purchase. We will assume you purchased $50,000 worth of 5000 different stocks through index funds and held onto them for the full five years. Your investment doubles in just over nine years. After five years your portfolio would have risen to $73,072.00.

## *Stocks I*

| Year | Beginning Balance | Commission Paid | Total gain 8% | | Interest Earned | Ending Balance | |
|---|---|---|---|---|---|---|---|
| | $ 50,000.00 | $ 250.00 | | | | $ 49,750.00 | |
| 1 | $ 49,750.00 | | $ | 0.08 | $ 3,980.00 | $ 53,980.00 | |
| 2 | $ 53,980.00 | | $ | 0.08 | $ 4,318.40 | $ 58,298.40 | |
| 3 | $ 58,298.40 | | $ | 0.08 | $ 4,663.87 | $ 62,962.27 | |
| 4 | $ 62,962.27 | | $ | 0.08 | $ 5,036.98 | $ 67,999.25 | |
| 5 | $ 67,999.25 | | $ | 0.08 | $ 5,439.94 | $ 73,439.19 | |
| | $ 73,439.19 | $ 367.20 | | | | $ 73,072.00 | After 5 years |
| 6 | $ 73,439.19 | | $ | 0.08 | $ 5,875.14 | $ 79,314.33 | |
| 7 | $ 79,314.33 | | $ | 0.08 | $ 6,345.15 | $ 85,659.48 | |
| 8 | $ 85,659.48 | | $ | 0.08 | $ 6,852.76 | $ 92,512.23 | |
| 9 | $ 92,512.23 | | $ | 0.08 | $ 7,400.98 | $ 99,913.21 | |
| 10 | $ 99,913.21 | | $ | 0.08 | $ 7,993.06 | $ 107,906.27 | |
| | $ 107,906.27 | $ 539.53 | | | | $ 107,366.74 | Doubled |

Table 3.3—Stocks I

# B U L L I O N

Bullion is gold or silver purchased (and priced) by weight, generally in ounces. Bullion has steep commissions and can exceed 10% in fees. For larger volumes we will assume a 5% fee. Thus, of your $50,000 investment, only $47,500 would actually have been left after you paid the commission. Gold increased 4.23% per year averaged between 1913 and 2010. By far the highest rates of increase were in the last three years. So, for this example the average is skewed dramatically but, we will still use the historical average … nobody has a crystal ball. Thus assuming it maintains this average annual increase of 4.23%, your investment will take 19 years to double and the value in your account after the five years in our experiment would be $55,511.24. Don't forget the commissions.

### *Bullion I*

| Year | Beginning Balance | Commission Paid | Interest 4.23% | Interest Earned | Ending Balance | |
|---|---|---|---|---|---|---|
| | $ 50,000.00 | $ 2,500.00 | | | $ 47,500.00 | |
| 1 | $ 47,500.00 | | $ | 0.04 | $ 2,009.25 | $ 49,509.25 | |
| 2 | $ 49,509.25 | | $ | 0.04 | $ 2,094.24 | $ 51,603.49 | |
| 3 | $ 51,603.49 | | $ | 0.04 | $ 2,182.83 | $ 53,786.32 | |
| 4 | $ 53,786.32 | | $ | 0.04 | $ 2,275.16 | $ 56,061.48 | |
| 5 | $ 56,061.48 | | $ | 0.04 | $ 2,371.40 | $ 58,432.88 | |
| | $ 58,432.88 | $ 2,921.64 | | | $ 55,511.24 | 5 Years |
| 6 | $ 58,432.88 | | $ | 0.04 | $ 2,471.71 | $ 60,904.59 | |
| 7 | $ 60,904.59 | | $ | 0.04 | $ 2,576.26 | $ 63,480.86 | |
| 8 | $ 63,480.86 | | $ | 0.04 | $ 2,685.24 | $ 66,166.10 | |
| 9 | $ 66,166.10 | | $ | 0.04 | $ 2,798.83 | $ 68,964.92 | |
| 10 | $ 68,964.92 | | $ | 0.04 | $ 2,917.22 | $ 71,882.14 | |
| 11 | $ 71,882.14 | | $ | 0.04 | $ 3,040.61 | $ 74,922.75 | |
| 12 | $ 74,922.75 | | $ | 0.04 | $ 3,169.23 | $ 78,091.99 | |
| 13 | $ 78,091.99 | | $ | 0.04 | $ 3,303.29 | $ 81,395.28 | |
| 14 | $ 81,395.28 | | $ | 0.04 | $ 3,443.02 | $ 84,838.30 | |
| 15 | $ 84,838.30 | | $ | 0.04 | $ 3,588.66 | $ 88,426.96 | |
| 16 | $ 88,426.96 | | $ | 0.04 | $ 3,740.46 | $ 92,167.42 | |
| 17 | $ 92,167.42 | | $ | 0.04 | $ 3,898.68 | $ 96,066.10 | |
| 18 | $ 96,066.10 | | $ | 0.04 | $ 4,063.60 | $ 100,129.69 | |
| 19 | $ 100,129.69 | | $ | 0.04 | $ 4,235.49 | $ 104,365.18 | |
| | $ 104,365.18 | $ 5,218.26 | | | $ 99,146.92 | Doubled |

Table 3.4—Bullion I

# REAL ESTATE

Income-producing real estate is unique. So, to ensure I am not sounding biased here, first and foremost it will cost you $5,000 of your $50,000 investment just to make the purchase. This high-priced fee is affectionately known as the closing costs. That means you only have $45,000 to invest in the first place. Again, as in all the examples above, there are many other things that can be done to offset this, but to keep the comparison simple we'll run with this flat number. We will also use the straight inflation rate which averaged about 3% since 1913 and therefore, the value of your property would double in 24 years. Well not exactly, the investment *will* double, but not with those closing costs attached. To recover those will take considerably longer. At the end of our five year cycle you would have <u>lost</u> money, ending with a balance of only $47,167.33. After the commissions are paid, your investment will take 34 years to double.

## *Real Estate I*

| Year | Beginning Balance | Commission Paid | Gain in Value @ 3% | Ending Balance | |
|---|---|---|---|---|---|
| | $ 50,000.00 | $ 5,000.00 | | $ 45,000.00 | |
| 1 | $ 45,000.00 | | $ 1,350.00 | $ 46,350.00 | |
| 2 | $ 46,350.00 | | $ 1,390.50 | $ 47,740.50 | |
| 3 | $ 47,740.50 | | $ 1,432.22 | $ 49,172.72 | |
| 4 | $ 49,172.72 | | $ 1,475.18 | $ 50,647.90 | |
| 5 | $ 50,647.90 | | $ 1,519.44 | $ 52,167.33 | After 5 years |
| | $ 52,167.33 | $ 5,000.00 | | $ 47,167.33 | After commission |
| 6 | $ 47,167.33 | | $ 1,415.02 | $ 48,582.35 | |
| 7 | $ 48,582.35 | | $ 1,457.47 | $ 50,039.82 | |
| 8 | $ 50,039.82 | | $ 1,501.19 | $ 51,541.02 | |
| 9 | $ 51,541.02 | | $ 1,546.23 | $ 53,087.25 | |
| 10 | $ 53,087.25 | | $ 1,592.62 | $ 54,679.87 | |
| 11 | $ 54,679.87 | | $ 1,640.40 | $ 56,320.26 | |
| 12 | $ 56,320.26 | | $ 1,689.61 | $ 58,009.87 | |
| 13 | $ 58,009.87 | | $ 1,740.30 | $ 59,750.17 | |
| 14 | $ 59,750.17 | | $ 1,792.51 | $ 61,542.67 | |
| 15 | $ 61,542.67 | | $ 1,846.28 | $ 63,388.95 | |

| | | | | | |
|---|---|---|---|---|---|
| 16 | $ 63,388.95 | | $ | 1,901.67 | $ 65,290.62 |
| 17 | $ 65,290.62 | | $ | 1,958.72 | $ 67,249.34 |
| 18 | $ 67,249.34 | | $ | 2,017.48 | $ 69,266.82 |
| 19 | $ 69,266.82 | | $ | 2,078.00 | $ 71,344.82 |
| 20 | $ 71,344.82 | | $ | 2,140.34 | $ 73,485.17 |
| 21 | $ 73,485.17 | | $ | 2,204.56 | $ 75,689.72 |
| 22 | $ 75,689.72 | | $ | 2,270.69 | $ 77,960.42 |
| 23 | $ 77,960.42 | | $ | 2,338.81 | $ 80,299.23 |
| 24 | $ 80,299.23 | | $ | 2,408.98 | $ 82,708.20 |
| 25 | $ 82,708.20 | | $ | 2,481.25 | $ 85,189.45 |
| 26 | $ 85,189.45 | | $ | 2,555.68 | $ 87,745.13 |
| 27 | $ 87,745.13 | | $ | 2,632.35 | $ 90,377.49 |
| 28 | $ 90,377.49 | | $ | 2,711.32 | $ 93,088.81 |
| 29 | $ 93,088.81 | | $ | 2,792.66 | $ 95,881.48 |
| 30 | $ 95,881.48 | | $ | 2,876.44 | $ 98,757.92 |
| 31 | $ 98,757.92 | | $ | 2,962.74 | $ 101,720.66 |
| 32 | $ 101,720.66 | | $ | 3,051.62 | $ 104,772.28 |
| 33 | $ 104,772.28 | | $ | 3,143.17 | $ 107,915.45 |
| 34 | $ 107,915.45 | | $ | 3,237.46 | $ 111,152.91 |
| | $ 111,152.91 | $ 10,000.00 | | | $ 101,152.91 |

Table 3.5—Real Estate I

# MONEY DOUBLING SUMMARY

So to recap, and keeping everything equal, the doubling of the selected investment vehicles would be as follows:

- Stocks would double your investment in just over 9 years.

- Bonds would double your money in 15 years.

- Bullion would require 19 years to double.

- Cash would also take 19 years.

- Real estate would take you 34 years before doubling.

There are other considerations that must be factored in and we'll take a look at the single most important first—a little something affectionately known as "Other People's Money," or OPM for short.

This is exactly what it sounds like. This is where folks borrow funds from other people to use in making a larger initial investment than would otherwise be possible using their own funds alone. How this works is in essence you borrow money against the asset you are buying. Essentially the use of OPM allows you to borrow money, pay interest for the use of that money, but make a larger investment than you would otherwise have been able to. You make money simply in the difference between the interest rate on the funds you have borrowed and the interest rate you are receiving, commonly known as "the spread." This is a bit of a gamble here as the investments you buy don't always perform as desired. Let's go back, in order, and apply OPM (or margin) to our examples beginning again with cash.

## OPM AND CASH

Banks are in the business of making money. They make some of it by charging borrowers higher interest rates for lending than they pay to get the funds they lend. You very well could borrow money via personal loan and use those funds for making a deposit into your savings account, but you would not be able to make more interest on the deposit of those funds than you would on the payment of interest on the borrowed funds. This in itself eliminates any possibility of margin buying or using OPM for any cash accounts. OPM is out for cash investments. Therefore your cash investment is stuck at 3.9%. Your investment would still take 19 years to double and you would still have the same $60,540.74 after five years.

## OPM AND BONDS

Many bonds cannot be purchased with any margin. However, there are a few that can. Some government bonds can be purchased with margins between 2% and 12% of the value of the bonds, some municipal bonds as high as 35%, and strong corporate convertible bonds can go as high as 50%. The stronger the financial backing of the company issuing the bond, the lower the interest rate they have to pay to get them sold. For this experiment we'll borrow money at 4% interest on bonds that will pay us 5% and we will borrow half of the amount we are investing for a 50% margin. It may not be likely that we could actually achieve these rates, but it is my example and I want to paint a positive picture for you!

So what happens in such an investment? This would net you nearly $2,000.00 above the first bond example (Table 1.2 above) and that's a little better return. There are lots and lots of assumptions and variables within this which we will not delve into, but suffice it to say that this is not a typical scenario. Rather, our "perfect world example" is for illustration only. However, if you could manage to put this together and do this continuously, you would now double your $50,000 in 14 years. Assuming you were able to make it work over five years, your net at the end of the fifth year would be $65,477.72 after returning the borrowed funds. You would have received about 5.14% on your 5% investment, and that is the example that needs to be understood.

## Bonds II

| Year | Beginning Balance | Margined 50% | Interest Paid @ 4% | Commission Paid (0.005%) | Interest rate earned 5% | Interest Amount earned | Ending Balance |
|---|---|---|---|---|---|---|---|
| | $ 50,000.00 | $ 25,000.00 | | | | | $ 75,000.00 |
| | $ 75,000.00 | | | $ 375.00 | | | $ 74,625.00 |
| 1 | $ 74,625.00 | | | | $ 0.05 | $ 3,731.25 | $ 78,356.25 |
| 2 | $ 78,356.25 | | $ 1,000.00 | | $ 0.05 | $ 3,917.81 | $ 81,274.06 |
| 3 | $ 81,274.06 | | $ 1,000.00 | | $ 0.05 | $ 4,063.70 | $ 84,337.77 |
| 4 | $ 84,337.77 | | $ 1,000.00 | | $ 0.05 | $ 4,216.89 | $ 87,554.65 |
| 5 | $ 87,554.65 | | $ 1,000.00 | | $ 0.05 | $ 4,377.73 | $ 90,932.39 |
| | $ 90,932.39 | | | $ 454.66 | After 5 years | | $ 90,477.72 |
| | | $ 25,000.00 | | | After return of margin | | $ 65,477.72 |
| 6 | $ 90,932.39 | | $ 1,000.00 | | $ 0.05 | $ 4,546.62 | $ 94,479.01 |
| 7 | $ 94,479.01 | | $ 1,000.00 | | $ 0.05 | $ 4,723.95 | $ 98,202.96 |
| 8 | $ 98,202.96 | | $ 1,000.00 | | $ 0.05 | $ 4,910.15 | $ 102,113.10 |
| 9 | $ 102,113.10 | | $ 1,000.00 | | $ 0.05 | $ 5,105.66 | $ 106,218.76 |
| 10 | $ 106,218.76 | | $ 1,000.00 | | $ 0.05 | $ 5,310.94 | $ 110,529.70 |
| 11 | $ 110,529.70 | | $ 1,000.00 | | $ 0.05 | $ 5,526.48 | $ 115,056.18 |
| 12 | $ 115,056.18 | | $ 1,000.00 | | $ 0.05 | $ 5,752.81 | $ 119,808.99 |
| 13 | $ 119,808.99 | | $ 1,000.00 | | $ 0.05 | $ 5,990.45 | $ 124,799.44 |
| 14 | $ 124,799.44 | | $ 1,000.00 | | $ 0.05 | $ 6,239.97 | $ 130,039.41 |
| | | $ 25,000.00 | $ 1,000.00 | $ 650.20 | After return of margin | | $ 103,389.22 |

Table 3.6—Bonds II

# O P M   A N D   S T O C K S

Margin accounts are considerably more prevalent in trading stocks. With a good margin account, you can buy $100,000 worth of good select stock with your $50,000 investment so long as the stocks are strong and meet several other parameters. But the stock market is immensely more volatile than the bond market, and the longer the time frame the more apt there is to be a surprise that throws our example to the wind. But, in the name of fairness, we will again use the same parameters (our "perfect world scenario") of borrowing at 4% and buying the same stock in our previous example. You would be receiving dividends and growth on stock worth $100,000 and paying off a loan for half of the original amount at the end. Left over for you would be $83,792.62. If you were to continue this process you would double your money in seven years. Word of caution here, if your investments fail to perform as you hope, you will still repay the loan, even if you have to borrow money to do it.

### *Stocks II*

| Year | Beginning Balance | Margined 100% | Interest Paid @ 4% | Commission Paid | Growth and dividends 8% | Growth achieved | Ending Balance |
|---|---|---|---|---|---|---|---|
| | $ 50,000.00 | $ 50,000.00 | | | | | $ 100,000.00 |
| | $ 100,000.00 | | | $ 500.00 | | | $ 99,500.00 |
| 1 | $ 99,500.00 | | $ 2,000.00 | | $ 0.08 | $ 7,960.00 | $ 105,460.00 |
| 2 | $ 105,460.00 | | $ 2,000.00 | | $ 0.08 | $ 8,436.80 | $ 111,896.80 |
| 3 | $ 111,896.80 | | $ 2,000.00 | | $ 0.08 | $ 8,951.74 | $ 118,848.54 |
| 4 | $ 118,848.54 | | $ 2,000.00 | | $ 0.08 | $ 9,507.88 | $ 126,356.43 |
| 5 | $ 126,356.43 | | $ 2,000.00 | | $ 0.08 | $ 10,108.51 | $ 134,464.94 |
| | $ 134,464.94 | | | $ 672.32 | | After 5 years | $ 133,792.62 |
| | | $ 50,000.00 | | | | After return of margin | $ 83,792.62 |
| 6 | $ 134,464.94 | | $ 2,000.00 | | $ 0.08 | $ 10,757.20 | $ 143,222.14 |
| 7 | $ 143,222.14 | | $ 2,000.00 | | $ 0.08 | $ 11,457.77 | $ 152,679.91 |
| | | $ 50,000.00 | | $ 763.40 | | After return of margin | $ 101,916.51 |

Table 3.7—Stocks II

# OPM AND GOLD

Gold, in our example, being the bullion itself and not any form of futures or exchange traded fund consisting of gold therefore has similar constraints as cash. Borrow money and buy bars, but don't ask for $100,000 worth of bars when sending a $50,000 check, you won't get it. The history of bullion since 1913 (with the exception of the last several years) has been dismal at best and often below the inflation rate. Borrowing margin money would cost you more than the return and you would end up losing more than you gained in the end, so there is no option other than the original one described above in Table 1.4.

# OPM AND REAL ESTATE

Real estate will allow high margin buying. Although the rules have changed dramatically after the crash in the mortgage market, it is expected that the $50,000 you are investing represents but a portion of the total purchase being made. In most cases today, after the housing crash beginning in 2008, banks will now want 20% or more down. From a different perspective that means the initial value of the purchase is five times the down payment. In our example $40,000 will secure a $200,000 property (the $45K we invested in Table 1.5 was reduced to $40K as closing costs are higher as property values increase).

There is something else a little different as well. Real estate, like cash in the bank, has appreciated at a lower percentage than bonds or stocks. But unlike stocks and bonds, you can readily borrow to purchase it. So, as we have with everything previous to this, we will keep this fair as well. If you were to purchase a property using the same appreciation rate and factoring in increasing values to include the borrowed funds (as with bonds and stocks), you have at the end of your five years, $61,854.81 after interest and commissions and the return of the mortgage (margin) are paid. This would take 11 years to double.

## Real Estate II

| Year | Beginning Balance | Commission Paid | Margined x 4 | Gain in Value @ 3% | Ending value | Interest Paid @ 4% | Ending Balance | |
|---|---|---|---|---|---|---|---|---|
| | $ 50,000.00 | $ 10,000.00 | | | | | $ 40,000.00 | |
| | $ 40,000.00 | | $ 160,000.00 | | | | $ 200,000.00 | |
| 1 | $ 200,000.00 | | | $ 6,000.00 | $ 206,000.00 | $ 6,400.00 | $ 199,600.00 | |
| 2 | $ 206,000.00 | | | $ 6,180.00 | $ 212,180.00 | $ 6,400.00 | $ 205,780.00 | |
| 3 | $ 212,180.00 | | | $ 6,365.40 | $ 218,545.40 | $ 6,400.00 | $ 212,145.40 | |
| 4 | $ 218,545.40 | | | $ 6,556.36 | $ 225,101.76 | $ 6,400.00 | $ 218,701.76 | |
| 5 | $ 225,101.76 | | | $ 6,753.05 | $ 231,854.81 | $ 6,400.00 | $ 225,454.81 | |
| | $ 231,854.81 | $ 10,000.00 | | | $ 231,854.81 | | $ 221,854.81 | After 5 years & commission |
| | $ 221,854.81 | | $ 160,000.00 | | | | $ 61,854.81 | After return of margin |
| 6 | $ 231,854.81 | | | $ 6,955.64 | $ 238,810.46 | $ 6,400.00 | $ 232,410.46 | |
| 7 | $ 238,810.46 | | | $ 7,164.31 | $ 245,974.77 | $ 6,400.00 | $ 239,574.77 | |
| 8 | $ 245,974.77 | | | $ 7,379.24 | $ 253,354.02 | $ 6,400.00 | $ 246,954.02 | |
| 9 | $ 253,354.02 | | | $ 7,600.62 | $ 260,954.64 | $ 6,400.00 | $ 254,554.64 | |
| 10 | $ 260,954.64 | | | $ 7,828.64 | $ 268,783.28 | $ 6,400.00 | $ 262,383.28 | |
| 11 | $ 268,783.28 | | | $ 8,063.50 | $ 276,846.77 | $ 6,400.00 | $ 270,446.77 | |
| | $ 276,846.77 | $ 10,000.00 | $ 160,000.00 | | | | $ 106,846.77 | |

Table 3.8—Real Estate II

Looking at the positions once again, factoring "margin buying" or the use of OPM gives a different result. Since cash and bullion do not incorporate margin buying there is no change.

- ❧ Stocks can double your money in as little as seven years
- ❧ Real estate will take 11 years to double
- ❧ Bonds will double you up in 14 years
- ❧ Cash and bullion still mosey along at 19 years each.

These figures do not make Real Estate very attractive as an investment but, there are inherent curiosities that need to be examined before we go to the next step in the equation. The biggest is the lender itself. Banks, as we stated, are in the business of making money. If life was truly as we suggest in the examples stated here, why then will banks lend but a maximum of but 50% on margin accounts for bonds, 100% on stocks but will automatically lend 400% (and in some cases much more) on income real estate?

First and foremost is the value of the instrument. Bonds and stocks are only as good as the company, state or municipality that issues them. If they default on the payment the game is over, and there will be little of value left to take to cover the bank's losses. Companies that issue stock are in exactly the same situation except that bond holders are paid before stock holders if there is a bankruptcy. Real estate has a very real value that can be seen, touched, and used. Even if the building (formally known as an improvement) is totally lost due to fire, flood, etc. it can be replaced with proper insurance.

> **Bonds and stocks are only as good as the company, state, or municipality that issues them.**

There is one other fundamental underlying reason. The interest on the margin purchase of the bonds and on the stocks is paid for in our examples out of the annual gains with the borrowed amount returned at the end of the holding period. In our real estate example, which we kept exactly the same for the sake of comparison, this is very different from reality. That difference is what we will look at next.

For this next round of comparison, we are going to make the assumption that income generated from the income producing real estate exactly equals the total expenses the property incurs each month. In other words, it is a totally break-even investment and will not add to or take from your personal monthly income.

Let's look at exactly the same investment once again, but this time instead of paying the interest annually as you did with stocks and bonds, your tenants will have been paying it for you each month. For the sake of saving time, we added the principal portion of a typical 30 year fixed rate mortgage at 4% interest. At the end of the very same five years your bill would not be the $160,000 after having made annual interest only payments. In this case the annual payments would have climbed to $9,166.32 (interest on the borrowed funds plus principal as established in a standard loan).

The balance to be paid back at the end of the five years would only be $144,996.56. That's a $15,003.44 difference and your investment now would be valued at a total of $76,858.25. You would now double your money just behind stocks in eight years.

## Real Estate III

| Year | Beginning Balance | Commission Paid | Margined x 4 | Gain in Value @ 3% | Income Received | Principal & Interest Paid @ 5% | Ending Balance | |
|---|---|---|---|---|---|---|---|---|
| | $ 50,000.00 | $ 10,000.00 | | | | | $ 40,000.00 | |
| | $ 40,000.00 | | $ 160,000.00 | | | | $ 200,000.00 | |
| 1 | $ 200,000.00 | | | $ 6,000.00 | $ 9,135.92 | 9,135.92 | $ 206,000.00 | |
| 2 | $ 206,000.00 | | | $ 6,180.00 | $ 9,135.92 | 9,135.92 | $ 212,180.00 | |
| 3 | $ 212,180.00 | | | $ 6,365.40 | $ 9,135.92 | 9,135.92 | $ 218,545.40 | |
| 4 | $ 218,545.40 | | | $ 6,556.36 | $ 9,135.92 | 9,135.92 | $ 225,101.76 | |
| 5 | $ 225,101.76 | | | $ 6,753.05 | $ 9,135.92 | 9,135.92 | $ 231,854.81 | |
| | $ 231,854.81 | $ 10,000.00 | | | | | $ 221,854.81 | 5 years & commission |
| | $ 221,854.81 | | $ 144,996.56 | | | | $ 76,858.25 | After return of margin |
| 6 | $ 231,854.81 | | | $ 6,955.64 | $ 9,135.92 | 9,135.92 | $ 238,810.46 | |
| 7 | $ 238,810.46 | | | $ 7,164.31 | $ 9,135.92 | 9,135.92 | $ 245,974.77 | |
| 8 | $ 245,974.77 | | | $ 7,379.24 | $ 9,135.92 | 9,135.92 | $ 253,354.02 | |
| | $ 253,354.02 | $ 10,000.00 | | | | | $ 243,354.02 | |
| | $ 243,354.02 | | 140,712.43 | | | | $ 102,641.59 | Doubled |

Table 3.9—Real Estate III

# THE GOVERNMENT FACTOR

We are going to look at just one more factor in our comparative equation. This last section will consider the government's role in our investments in terms of taxes, and it is where things begin to get interesting.

Interest income is taxable. Stock dividends are, in essence, a form of interest in the eyes of the government and are taxed at both state and federal levels. Capital gains are taxable—when real estate or stocks increase in value above the price that was paid it is a capital gain in both cases. Rental income is taxable. It's actually getting pretty hard to find something that is not taxable. But there is a little something out there for us.

For this example we will consider the 15% tax bracket and we will use the same rates of return as we started with, what bracket you are in does not matter for the example. Do the calculation on your own.

We will take one last look at the other investments from a tax standpoint before we leave them for good. Our cash investment interest earned in the example (from Table 1.9) would have cost you $1,263.75 leaving you with $58,885.48. It would reduce your overall actual gain to 3.27% and will therefore double, not in 19 years, but in 22 years.

## Cash II

| Year | Beginning Balance | Interest 3.9% | Interest Earned | Tax @ 15% | Taxes Paid | Actual Gain | Ending Balance | |
|---|---|---|---|---|---|---|---|---|
| 1 | $ 50,000.00 | 0.04 | $ 1,950.00 | 0.15 | $ 292.50 | $ 1,657.50 | $ 51,657.50 | |
| 2 | $ 51,657.50 | 0.04 | $ 2,014.64 | 0.15 | $ 302.20 | $ 1,712.45 | $ 53,369.95 | |
| 3 | $ 53,369.95 | 0.04 | $ 2,081.43 | 0.15 | $ 312.21 | $ 1,769.21 | $ 55,139.16 | |
| 4 | $ 55,139.16 | 0.04 | $ 2,150.43 | 0.15 | $ 322.56 | $ 1,827.86 | $ 56,967.02 | |
| 5 | $ 56,967.02 | 0.04 | $ 2,221.71 | 0.15 | $ 333.26 | $ 1,888.46 | $ 58,855.48 | After 5 years |
| 6 | $ 58,855.48 | 0.04 | $ 2,295.36 | 0.15 | $ 344.30 | $ 1,951.06 | $ 60,806.54 | |
| 7 | $ 60,806.54 | 0.04 | $ 2,371.46 | 0.15 | $ 355.72 | $ 2,015.74 | $ 62,822.28 | |
| 8 | $ 62,822.28 | 0.04 | $ 2,450.07 | 0.15 | $ 367.51 | $ 2,082.56 | $ 64,904.83 | |
| 9 | $ 64,904.83 | 0.04 | $ 2,531.29 | 0.15 | $ 379.69 | $ 2,151.60 | $ 67,056.43 | |
| 10 | $ 67,056.43 | 0.04 | $ 2,615.20 | 0.15 | $ 392.28 | $ 2,222.92 | $ 69,279.35 | |
| 11 | $ 69,279.35 | 0.04 | $ 2,701.89 | 0.15 | $ 405.28 | $ 2,296.61 | $ 71,575.96 | |
| 12 | $ 71,575.96 | 0.04 | $ 2,791.46 | 0.15 | $ 418.72 | $ 2,372.74 | $ 73,948.70 | |
| 13 | $ 73,948.70 | 0.04 | $ 2,884.00 | 0.15 | $ 432.60 | $ 2,451.40 | $ 76,400.10 | |
| 14 | $ 76,400.10 | 0.04 | $ 2,979.60 | 0.15 | $ 446.94 | $ 2,532.66 | $ 78,932.77 | |
| 15 | $ 78,932.77 | 0.04 | $ 3,078.38 | 0.15 | $ 461.76 | $ 2,616.62 | $ 81,549.39 | |
| 16 | $ 81,549.39 | 0.04 | $ 3,180.43 | 0.15 | $ 477.06 | $ 2,703.36 | $ 84,252.75 | |
| 17 | $ 84,252.75 | 0.04 | $ 3,285.86 | 0.15 | $ 492.88 | $ 2,792.98 | $ 87,045.73 | |
| 18 | $ 87,045.73 | 0.04 | $ 3,394.78 | 0.15 | $ 509.22 | $ 2,885.57 | $ 89,931.29 | |
| 19 | $ 89,931.29 | 0.04 | $ 3,507.32 | 0.15 | $ 526.10 | $ 2,981.22 | $ 92,912.52 | |
| 20 | $ 92,912.52 | 0.04 | $ 3,623.59 | 0.15 | $ 543.54 | $ 3,080.05 | $ 95,992.57 | |
| 21 | $ 95,992.57 | 0.04 | $ 3,743.71 | 0.15 | $ 561.56 | $ 3,182.15 | $ 99,174.72 | |
| 22 | $ 99,174.72 | 0.04 | $ 3,867.81 | 0.15 | $ 580.17 | $ 3,287.64 | $ 102,462.36 | Doubled |

Table 3.10—Cash II

Your bond investment interest will now be worth $61,513.56 in five years and will take 18 years to double.

### Bonds III

| Year | Beginning Balance | Margined 50% | Interest Paid @ 4% | Commission Paid | Interest 5% | Interest Earned | Tax paid @ 15% | Ending Balance | |
|---|---|---|---|---|---|---|---|---|---|
| | $ 50,000.00 | $ 25,000.00 | | | | | | $ 75,000.00 | |
| | $ 75,000.00 | | | $ 375.00 | | | | $ 74,625.00 | |
| 1 | $ 74,625.00 | | $ 1,000.00 | | 0.05 | $ 3,731.25 | $ 559.69 | $ 76,796.56 | |
| 2 | $ 76,796.56 | | $ 1,000.00 | | 0.05 | $ 3,839.83 | $ 575.97 | $ 79,060.42 | |
| 3 | $ 79,060.42 | | $ 1,000.00 | | 0.05 | $ 3,953.02 | $ 592.95 | $ 81,420.48 | |
| 4 | $ 81,420.48 | | $ 1,000.00 | | 0.05 | $ 4,071.02 | $ 610.65 | $ 83,880.85 | |
| 5 | $ 83,880.85 | | $ 1,000.00 | | 0.05 | $ 4,194.04 | $ 629.11 | $ 86,445.79 | |
| | $ 86,445.79 | $ 25,000.00 | | $ 432.23 | | | | $ 61,013.56 | 5 Years After return of margin |
| 6 | $ 86,445.79 | | $ 1,000.00 | | 0.05 | $ 4,322.29 | $ 648.34 | $ 89,119.74 | |
| 7 | $ 89,119.74 | | $ 1,000.00 | | 0.05 | $ 4,455.99 | $ 668.40 | $ 91,907.33 | |
| 8 | $ 91,907.33 | | $ 1,000.00 | | 0.05 | $ 4,595.37 | $ 689.30 | $ 94,813.39 | |
| 9 | $ 94,813.39 | | $ 1,000.00 | | 0.05 | $ 4,740.67 | $ 711.10 | $ 97,842.96 | |
| 10 | $ 97,842.96 | | $ 1,000.00 | | 0.05 | $ 4,892.15 | $ 733.82 | $ 101,001.28 | |
| 11 | $ 101,001.28 | | $ 1,000.00 | | 0.05 | $ 5,050.06 | $ 757.51 | $ 104,293.84 | |
| 12 | $ 104,293.84 | | $ 1,000.00 | | 0.05 | $ 5,214.69 | $ 782.20 | $ 107,726.32 | |
| 13 | $ 107,726.32 | | $ 1,000.00 | | 0.05 | $ 5,214.69 | $ 782.20 | $ 111,158.81 | |
| 14 | $ 111,158.81 | | $ 1,000.00 | | 0.05 | $ 5,214.69 | $ 782.20 | $ 114,591.30 | |
| 15 | $ 114,591.30 | | $ 1,000.00 | | 0.05 | $ 5,214.69 | $ 782.20 | $ 118,023.79 | |
| 16 | $ 118,023.79 | | $ 1,000.00 | | 0.05 | $ 5,214.69 | $ 782.20 | $ 121,456.28 | |
| 17 | $ 121,456.28 | | $ 1,000.00 | | 0.05 | $ 5,214.69 | $ 782.20 | $ 124,888.76 | |
| 18 | $ 124,888.76 | $ 25,000.00 | $ 1,000.00 | $ 641.61 | 0.05 | $ 5,214.69 | $ 782.20 | $ 128,321.25 | |
| | | | | | | | | $ 101,679.65 | After return of margin |

Table 3.11—Bonds III

Bullion is too erratically priced to predict, but the same capital gains rules apply as to stock. Taking the long term capital gain approach average and reducing the amount you get back from the commissions paid for the transactions, you would be doubling your money in 42 years walking away with a net gain of only $646.00. Bullion is only for established wealth to hedge against inflation for the long term, it will not make you wealthy.

Your 8% return on stocks is generally a combination of dividends and capital gains. Dividends are similar to interest for tax purposes. Capital gains is the difference in the price of the stock at the time you bought it and the price at the time you sold it. If you bought a share for $50.00 and sold it for $60.00 your capital gain is the $10.00 difference.

You can easily have a capital loss but we will assume for the example you had a gain. You don't pay tax on capital gains until the stock is sold, but you will on dividends, so each must be calculated separately. Since we said that the overall rate of return each year was 8% we will divide that accordingly. Dividends we will say represents 3% of the equation and 5% is the added value of the stock.

Think of this added value as a combination of two separate components, half for inflation of the company's assets and half for investments the company makes in itself, doesn't matter what percentages are used, but combined it becomes the capital gain. Thus, of the 8% total return, 3% of it is taxable at 15% as dividends paid out to you, the stock holder reducing your overall gain by $2,238.75. The other 5% is taxed at the capital gains rate, (which just happens to be 15% for the folks in this example). In this case your investment would double in eight years and at the end of the five years you would have $79,581.91.

## Stocks III

| Year | Beginning Balance | Margined 100% | Interest Paid @ 4% | Commission Paid | Increase 10 value = 8% | Increased Value | Tax paid @ 15% | Ending Balance | |
|---|---|---|---|---|---|---|---|---|---|
| | $ 50,000.00 | $ 50,000.00 | | | | | | $ 100,000.00 | |
| | $ 100,000.00 | | | $ 500.00 | | | | $ 99,500.00 | |
| 1 | $ 99,500.00 | | | | 0.08 | $ 7,960.00 | $ 447.75 | $ 107,012.25 | |
| 2 | $ 107,012.25 | | $ 2,000.00 | | 0.08 | $ 8,560.98 | $ 481.56 | $ 113,091.67 | |
| 3 | $ 113,091.67 | | $ 2,000.00 | | 0.08 | $ 9,047.33 | $ 508.91 | $ 119,630.10 | |
| 4 | $ 119,630.10 | | $ 2,000.00 | | 0.08 | $ 9,570.41 | $ 538.34 | $ 126,662.17 | |
| 5 | $ 126,662.17 | | $ 2,000.00 | | 0.08 | $ 10,132.97 | $ 569.98 | $ 134,225.16 | |
| | $ 134,225.16 | $ 50,000.00 | $ 2,000.00 | $ 671.13 | | ** | $ 1,972.13 | $ 131,554.04 | After 5 years |
| | | | | | | | | $ 81,554.04 | After return of margin |
| | | | | | | | | $ 79,581.91 | After capital gains tax |
| 6 | $ 134,225.16 | | $ 2,000.00 | | 0.08 | $ 10,738.01 | $ 604.01 | $ 142,359.16 | |
| 7 | $ 142,359.16 | | $ 2,000.00 | | 0.08 | $ 11,388.73 | $ 640.62 | $ 151,107.28 | |
| 8 | $ 151,107.28 | | $ 2,000.00 | | 0.08 | $ 12,088.58 | $ 679.98 | $ 160,515.88 | |
| | | $ 50,000.00 | $ 2,000.00 | $ 802.58 | | ** | $ (6,907.24) | $ 100,806.06 | After return of margin |

\* 3% of the increase is dividends, 5% is capital gains, thus .375 of the 8% is taxed at 15% tax rate as annual income

\*\* 5% is capital gains, thus .625 of the increased value is taxed upon sale, also at 15%

A 30% tax bracket would have a greater impact

Table 3.12—Stocks III

Remember, this comparison is meant for illustration purposes only, not to be looked at as an exact science. The fact that the interest rates are nearly identical after doubling down on the stock purchase with a high risk margin account is not entirely accurate. In a real world scenario, there would be taxes paid on the non-margined account, thereby reducing the value accordingly. It is in order, adding subsequent aspects as the idea expands. Our five year experiment is only to suggest the different aspects of possibilities, not to suggest strategies.

Real estate then becomes the odd ball. Simply put, the government cannot afford to shelter the populace of this county, it would go broke. Therefore, there are incentives designed to encourage you and me to help them do just that—the young, the old, those not quite established, middle class with college loans, those who relocate frequently due to job changes, and so on. These folks all need places to live and Uncle Sam sort of adopts you as a partner to get it done. How? By assuming the building you purchase will end up completely worthless over the next 30 years. Not the land upon which the building sits, just the building itself. For residential living the property or land is generally considered to be worth 20% of the total price paid. In our case the $200,000 property has a land value of $40,000 the building thus $160,000.

**Real estate is the odd ball investment—an odd partnership with Uncle Sam.**

This is the amount the government allows us to say will be worth nothing 30 years from now. So $160,000 divided by 30 years is $5,333 per year. What does that mean? As we said, things now get interesting. Let's assume you earn $60,000.00 a year at your job. You pay tax at 15%

and dutifully send a check to the government each year for $9,000 and he appreciates it, but you don't have to. The example we used above assumed that every dollar we collected in rent went back out in expenses in one form or another. There is still income from the property and that is calculated as the reduction in other taxes due to depreciation on your investment. In this case you are legally telling the government that you did not earn $60,000 but that you only actually earned $54,667. Therefore instead of paying $9,000 each year you will only write that check for $8,200.05.

Over the same five years you have saved $3,999.75 in taxes to the federal government on the money you received from your regular paying job because you bought a different type of investment vehicle. Now if you are like most people you don't write a check to pay your taxes at the end of the year, you select "married" and claim a few exemptions or whatever on your W-4 and let your payroll department take it away for you. You have to just love those payroll folks! But now you have the right to go in to that same payroll office and reduce your withholdings and have less money taken out each week, or don't, and receive a nice check back at the end of every year.

**Real estate investment saves you real money on your real tax bill.**

At the end of your five years you would have $76,829.51. You would double your money just behind stocks in eight years.

## Real Estate IV

| Year | Beginning Balance | Commission Paid | Margined x 4 | Gain in Value @ 3% | Income Received | Principal & Interest paid @ 4% | Sub Ending Balance | Deduction on income | Ending Balance |
|---|---|---|---|---|---|---|---|---|---|
| | $ 50,000.00 | $ 10,000.00 | | | | | $ 40,000.00 | | |
| | $ 40,000.00 | | $ 160,000.00 | | | | $ 200,000.00 | | |
| 1 | $ 200,000.00 | | | $ 6,000.00 | $ 9,406.32 | $ 9,406.32 | $ 206,000.00 | $ 800.00 | $ 206,800.00 |
| 2 | $ 206,000.00 | | | $ 6,180.00 | $ 9,406.32 | $ 9,406.32 | $ 212,180.00 | $ 800.00 | $ 212,980.00 |
| 3 | $ 212,180.00 | | | $ 6,365.40 | $ 9,406.32 | $ 9,406.32 | $ 218,545.40 | $ 800.00 | $ 219,345.40 |
| 4 | $ 218,545.40 | | | $ 6,556.36 | $ 9,406.32 | $ 9,406.32 | $ 225,101.76 | $ 800.00 | $ 225,901.76 |
| 5 | $ 225,101.76 | | | $ 6,753.05 | $ 9,406.32 | $ 9,406.32 | $ 231,854.81 | $ 800.00 | $ 232,654.81 |
| | $ 231,854.81 | $ 10,000.00 | | | | 5 yrs & comm. | $ 221,854.81 | | |
| | $ 221,854.81 | | $ 144,996.56 | | | Funds returned | $ 76,858.25 | $ 4,000.00 | $ 80,858.25 |
| | | | | | | less capital gains | $ 4,028.74 | | $ 76,829.51 |
| 6 | $ 231,854.81 | | | $ 6,955.64 | $ 9,406.32 | $ 9,406.32 | $ 238,810.46 | $ 800.00 | $ 239,610.46 |
| 7 | $ 238,810.46 | | | $ 7,164.31 | $ 9,406.32 | $ 9,406.32 | $ 245,974.77 | $ 800.00 | $ 246,774.77 |
| 8 | $ 245,974.77 | | | $ 7,379.24 | $ 9,406.32 | $ 9,406.32 | $ 253,354.02 | $ 800.00 | $ 254,154.02 |
| | $ 253,354.02 | $ 10,000.00 | 137,390.27 | | | $ (8,394.56) | $ 97,569.18 | | |
| | | | | | | capital gains | | | |

Table 3.13—Real Estate IV

Let's recap one last time in order of return, thus:

| Investment Type | Return | Doubled in ... |
|---|---|---|
| Stocks | $79,581.91 | 8 years |
| Income Producing Real Estate | $76,829.51 | 8 years |
| Bonds | $61,013.56 | 18 years |
| Cash | $58,855.48 | 22 years |
| Bullion | $55,511.24 | 42 years |

There are several additional things that go into the purchase of rental real estate that we will not get into in this section since I wanted everything to stay fair and equitable across the board. Understand that very few buyers will ever buy rental property without expecting to generate some cash monthly for their trouble. This is in addition to the growth of that investment which we have classified up to this point as a Return On Investment (ROI). Put money into something, get something out of it.

There is another entire section that pertains only to Income Producing Real Estate called Return On Equity (ROE) that we will look at in Chapter 14. None of the investment categories above offers this additional benefit although, as discussed earlier, stocks is a combination of the two. But Financial Planners live by the creed, "Thou shall never spend principal" couple that with the requirement to reinvest the dividends in order to get the returns shown and there is nothing to spend. Thus, for a very long time, there is nothing for you. This is perfect for people who earn 250k and a year and have learned to live on only 100k but most people are not in this group. Personally I think many people feel, if they can never spend it, why bother investing in anything. That thinking has a lot to do with society at large being engrossed in instant gratification and thinking exclusively of only today. But well selected Income Producing Real Estate will grow in value comparable to the best alternatives AND it will generate cash for you to enjoy. You can even use that cash to feed the other investment categories—stocks and bonds. We will look into this and the details required to ensure this is what actually happens after you close on the deal but there are still a couple of other important issues to cover first. This then, becomes your foundation for understanding, greatly simplified of course. The next question thus becomes, to whom do you go to for your investment advice?

# WHO CAN YOU TRUST?

I have found if you have a stock broker, you never mention you're considering purchasing real estate. He'll point out all the bad things about real estate and vehemently oppose the idea. Why? Two reasons, first he is not an expert in real estate. Second, the account he manages (yours) will drop by the amount of the investment you are making and that will reduce potential commissions to him from your account. In fact, if you told your stock broker you will be buying gold, bonds, or starting your own business you will get the same reaction: "You need me as your trained professional. Doctor's don't operate on themselves."

If you tell a financial planner these things you will get different answers, but for the same reasons. Some financial planners are unique and will recommend real estate in the portfolio, but many of those will recommend strongly against you making the purchase, rather (while pointing out all the terrible pitfalls of being a landlord) they will recommend REIT's. Instruments they are likely to sell.

Bond traders will lambast everything. Nothing is as secure as bonds, etc. etc. The more cash in your account the more commissions can be generated. Precious metals traders and real estate agent/brokers don't generally fall into this grouping. You buy precious metals via a phone call and tell the agent what you want, submit a check, and receive your investment a week later, along with an upfront fee of 10%. They'll deduct another 10% when you sell, and if you buy you will eventually sell— or your kids will when you pass on. Either way, they will get another commission. They would prefer you to sell soon by the way. Real estate works similarly, commissions on both ends. And when you buy, you will sell … but the differences are huge and we have only scratched the proverbial surface.

Every investment instrument has benefits and every investment instrument has detriments. Every sales agent for every possible investment will have their own spin. To each, every other investment choice but theirs will result in either disastrous consequences, or at least will be less viable for you than what they are selling. The only possible unbiased avenue for you to follow is to gain all the knowledge you can and become wholly responsible for your own actions.

We still haven't answered the question about who you go to for advice and there is still one more little thing to understand before we do. Although it is simple, it might not be too easy to grasp and it is this:

This is not about you!

When you speak with a financial advisor, know that it is not about you, it is about keeping you happy enough to continue generating commissions from your money. Real estate sales people will not show you a house for $200,000 if your income and budget readily allows you a $400,000 mortgage because their commission will be larger if they sell you what you can afford as opposed to what you tell them you want. Whatever price you want to pay is irrelevant. The first question they will ask you is "How much can you afford?" not "How much do you want to spend?" If everything you read tells you to put 5% into gold, the gold dealer will tell you that to properly cushion against the perils of inflation your portfolio should contain at least 10%. Stock brokers love day traders or anyone whose account they can or you will voluntarily churn. Financial planners often select the instruments that offer the biggest fee to the planner, not necessarily the highest rate of return for the customer. In many instances these planners managing your accounts accept a bonus, which in this case is another name for kickbacks, from the companies whose products they push you towards accepting into your accounts. So, who can you trust and where should you go?

You go to all of them!

Think about it, Lexus might win car of the year for four years straight, but do you think you could find a BMW dealer that will recommend buying a Lexus? Will a real estate agent recommend a retired couple with a large cash account rent instead of buy? Pushing the instruments they sell is natural and perfectly acceptable. They are sales people. Their job is to sell you something. Their income only manifest by their success. If they are successful they get paid, if they are not, they don't. Period. Don't blame them, they have children to feed just like you. It's up to you to know the rules of engagement.

The miracle on 34th Street does not apply to the financial sector. The only individual you can ever trust to make the correct decisions for you is you. The only way you can make the correct decisions is to have the knowledge necessary to make such decisions. Henry Ford was not cocky in his Senate hearing, he was profoundly confident of his ability to utilize his knowledge as an arsenal to, "… have it all back in three years." My late father-in-law kept a plaque on his wall that read: "It's not about how much you know—it's about how much you know, that just ain't so." The irony is that all you need to know is available for free. You simply need to do two things: first, understand the need for this knowledge, and second, the drive to get up off your… couch and go get it!

No one on the face of this planet will ever assume responsibility for what another person chooses to regard as fact or fiction. Nowhere is this truer than in the world of money and investing.

CHAPTER FOUR

# Foundations

T he primary focus of this book is on what I have found to be the correct way to research, purchase, and manage income producing real estate. I have been doing this part time for 31 years through good and bad markets, and it is what I am most comfortable with. Does that make me an expert in every category? Nope. In the appendix you will see another half dozen books recommended under this topic and each will bring some new consideration for you. I highly recommend a regimen of reading and diligent application of the ideas as you absorb them. It will not take long to garner an understanding for and perhaps gain a very different perspective than you might be accustomed.

Let's go back a ways to see why this might be the case.

For the most part we are taught from a very early age to work hard, study hard, get a good job, and make something of your life. When you land a good job with a great company and get vacation time, sick time, a few benefits, and a raise now and then, congratulations, you are among the masses. Whether you earn $15.00 or $250.00 per hour you are in the same boat in two very simple ways. You do not answer to yourself and your fate is in someone else's hands. One person scrapes by in his or her small apartment managing to get to work in the beat up old Ford Pinto every day for a $15.00 per hour salary. Up the hill in the five thousand square foot manor house with the S Series Mercedes prominently displayed on the cobbled drive lives the other earning $250.00 per hour. More likely than not, both are very similar, these folks are also just squeaking by, living paycheck to paycheck. Both will have debt exceeding their means, both will have consciously planned to escape the bonds restraining them from their problem, and neither will ever take action towards implementing those plans.

To help pay my way through the local community college I worked part-time as a salesman for Lawn Doctor in an upscale area of Rockland County in New York. This was a great company to work for at the time and probably still is today. They paid good commissions after prescreening potential customers and with a nudge in the right place, the product sold itself. But the one lesson I learned which I most covet today was least expected and perhaps most misunderstood then. An early Saturday call had taken me to a very large home perched on a hillside surrounded by others of equal grandeur. Six thousand square feet or so of Tudor style mansion-wanna-be complete with cobbled drive and the Mercedes displayed outside one of the three bay custom garage doors. It had a pool, a tennis court, beautiful drapes, and was completely and professionally landscaped with estate style grounds. It reeked of wealth. When I knocked on the door and announced my presence I was told, through the still closed door by a female voice, to "Go ahead and measure it up," which I did. Upon return I was told, again through the still closed door, to "Just send me a bill." At this point I politely told the voice that I could not do that. There were papers to be signed, that it would take but a few moments, and would she please open the door so we could conclude business.

There was an audible groan from within but the door did part a moment later. She had opened the door slightly, never looked at me, stuck her head out, looked left and then right and then motioned me to come in without letting go of the door knob and never opening it an inch more than necessary to allow me to literally squeeze inside. My perplexity and confusion were instantly explained upon entry as the only piece of furniture visible in the house was a card table and two folding chairs. The expensive drapes on the front of the house were the only items in the rooms facing the street. Nothing garnered the windows to the rear. Being young and naive I had assumed they had just moved in and their furniture was being shipped. That was instantly corrected after telling her how beautiful the property was. She told me they'd had it and the pool installed "last year." Being a little slow and stupid, I asked about the furniture anyway and was meekly told that they were "working on it." I walked out of that house with a commission she could ill afford to pay, but to this day I will attest that that was the single most guaranteed commission I would ever make. Her neighbors, it seemed, all had Lawn Doctor and be damned, she would too! Her neighbors could see the Lawn Doctor truck at the house five times a year. They could not see the furniture.

Should the individual earning $15.00 an hour lose that job the fall will not be from as high a perch as will the one losing the $250.00 an hour job. However, the time to make the plunge to rock bottom will eerily be about the same for both as neither will have the necessary wherewithal to prevent the catastrophe from occurring. I suggested reading *The Master Builder's* to see how far it is possible to climb. Read the same book to see how fast the fall can be.

It does not have to be this way. It is this way because of conditioning, the things we are repeatedly subjected to. This in concert with a profound lack of education on the matter of basic financial controls— in short, things no one taught us. We are surrounded and bombarded continuously with enticements to rid us of our hard earned cash. TV, magazines, billboards, all forms of electronic media, the Jones' as well as all the other neighbors all suggest the better life is at our fingertips—VISA and MasterCard accepted. Think about this for just one second, what is it that every single one of these ads wants of you? Regardless of what it is they are selling, promoting, suggesting, or giving away free … "just pay shipping and handling," what do they want?

It is your dollars.

It's not even *just* your dollars. The marketing mechanism for advertising dollars is equally huge. The competition for companies to advertise on this media or that are all pouring effort into the fray with claims they have the most readers, viewers, followers, particular age group, and the absolute highest level of influence possible for that particular demographic target you need to reach. They will even tell what your target should be for that widget you sell.

This country is a manufacturer's paradise!

This country is a consumer's paradise!

Which came first?

Consumerism is here to stay. Some suggest Henry Ford began the age of consumerism consciously changing advertising from "Buy a Ford, Save the Difference," to "Buy a Ford, Spend the Difference"[1] in 1928 after his assembly line made the Model "T" available to the masses at a consumer's price. The consumerism genie was out of the bottle, and it is not going to go back.

There are a great many true values out there for the things you need and want, but they need to be carefully sorted through. There are hundreds available of every conceivable item in every quality and price, and no, you do not need the "buy-one-get-one-free" special. You select from the available choices balancing price and quality to suit your needs. Some consumers will even research what they need or want, compare quality and features, select the brand and model they want, and then look for a sale before making the purchase to ensure they receive the best bargain. Many though, are impulse buyers, meaning they buy it as soon as they see it so long as they have cash or credit available, whether or not they need it not necessarily a consideration.

Everything is available and everybody involved in the sale of these products wants you to buy theirs. It therefore only stands to reason thus that in this country, people vigorously compete for your business. When someone can do something for you cheaper, or provide you with more service, or make you something better and for less, you will buy it. A deal is consummated and money is exchanged. Knowing what you need is your business. Convincing you to buy theirs is their business. The problem in this country is there is much more effort expended on the convincing part than in the knowing part. We are highly susceptible to impulses from a 139 billion dollar advertising industry in 2012.[2] If this were not true, a 30 second Super Bowl commercial would not cost $3,500,000.00.[3]

Now I know there are a lot of great things we need to live and you'll never get them for free, but use a little common sense. One of the best sources I have found for guidance in this area is Dr. Thomas J. Stanley, *The Millionaire Next Door*. Get his book, read it a few times, and practice his advice.

It's your money. You work hard for it. You should make those who want it work harder than you had to in earning it before they are able to get it from you.

**It's your money. You work hard for it. You should make those who want it work harder than you had to in earning it.**

# ORIGIN OF THE CREDIT RATING REVEALED

One other major piece of the financial foundation and the one place most every book on finance always seems to visit is the credit rating, but it is often misunderstood as well. It will be your best friend if you start a part-time career in Real Estate Investment and we need to take a look at that as well, but once again, from a slightly different perspective.

You can't get much in this world today without good credit. But before we get into the bowels of your personal credit situation, let's first take a look at why it's so important and to whom it is important. Remember that line at the end of the last chapter "It's not about you"? Recall also finding a niche and filling it in the competitive world of business today? Simply put, the seller doesn't want the item you are buying from him or her back. Lenders are willing to pay good money to see what those odds are based upon the level of historical financial commitment and respect you have for yourself and for others prior to consummating a deal with you.

Unless you are buying an item entirely for cash, there is a degree of a gamble for the lender and they will stack the odds in their favor with a credit report. Their interpretation of what is in those reports helps mitigate their risk. But credit reporting was not born to ensure the bank that your house, your car, your boat, train, or plane won't come back via repossession. It grew into what it is today from the days of the General Store running simple IOU tabs to its local patrons. To understand how credit reporting ended up the incredible force it is today requires an understanding of what a bank really is, and how it works. Try to stay with me here, we'll be back with a better understanding of credit reporting in a minute.

How does a bank actually work?

In short, a bank is a repository of funds collected and held securely for depositors and with the right to use these funds to lend to others who want it and can demonstrate a track record for repaying what they borrow. To entice you to make deposits into the bank, they offer interest at competitive rates or free toasters ... whatever it takes to get you to open an account. They pay you for depositing money and they lend your money to others. Clearly, you will never have deposited enough for them to make so much that lending your few dollars out will afford them that shiny glass tower in lower Manhattan. So how does it really work?

Let's say you open a savings account with a thousand dollar deposit, so do 177 others just like you. The bank now has an *asset pool* of $178,000. If you looked at the example of the mortgage in chapter three where we borrowed $160,000, you could think this is where that money comes from and you might be correct—to a point. The bank will lend you those same dollars for less than a day.

The money that has been deposited into the bank by the collective masses is known overall as an *asset*, and bank assets are defined in what can only be considered convoluted terms. Understanding this will become the basis for our using these same methods later.

Thus the bank, having accumulated these deposits, reports to the Federal Reserve that they now have an asset valued at $178,000 against which it would like to lend you money for your mortgage. The Federal Reserve agrees and gives the bank permission to lend between 90 and 97% (the maximum) of that asset. (We are using the lower end for our example 90%). In doing this the bank is allowed to lend the requested $160,000 and further allows the bank to immediately sell that loan to investors in the form of a bond. The interest rate the bank collects from you on the mortgage is always higher than the interest rate it pays on the bond he has sold. The difference, you may recall, is called the "spread" and is for the banks to do with as it pleases.

The bank receives money from the sale of the bonds, in this case $160,000, which becomes an asset against which the bank is allowed to lend.[4] So our $160,000 bond proceed is then converted, in the same fashion as the original deposits, to another lendable asset valued at 90% or $144,000. Once that money is lent another bond is sold and the process is repeated. The new $144k loan becoming an *asset*, money is borrowed, money is lent, bonds are sold etc., etc. This continues all the way down until nothing is left. In the end, our little collection of depositors with their little $1,000 pots was transformed into a collective *asset* pile worth about $1,750,000, minimum, using the 90% rule. The strength of the bank determines the allowable percentage and if a bank ranks at the top, this asset pile is worth closer to $5,000,000. Thus it pays for a bank to be careful. Each step in the process costs the bank a particular interest rate, and each step through the progression, the borrower pays a higher interest rate. From the money earned between the difference of these two interest rates (and the thousands of other transactions just like it), the bank can now afford their glass towers and the tellers within. So as you can see in our very simplified arrangement, it is a pyramid. The principals within are not terribly different from those used for building real estate empires.[5]

But before we get into all that, consider for a moment what might happen if we should default on our $160,000 mortgage. An entire pyramid worth $1,750,000 could be in jeopardy.

# THE IMPORTANCE OF CREDIT REPORTS

Now we can go back to credit reports. They evolved over time from their origins in General Stores, picked up by the banking industry to assist bankers in helping ensure the assets they were considering were safe. The "lists" of who paid and who did not were borrowed by the banks simply because it worked for the General Stores. Many of these borrowers were farmers who did not have steady income. Their bills could go many months without payment. As the banks evolved, they needed to make sound decisions. There was no Federal Reserve back then. Banks had to make decisions themselves as to whether or not you and your need for their money was sound and strong enough to support the lending you sought.

There was also no FDIC (Federal Deposit Insurance Corporation) or other guarantee agencies either. It truly was a matter of trust. The banking industry evolved rapidly and many laws and changes were made after the Depression, and the evolution continues with the process still being far from perfect. The S&L crisis of the 80s and 90s saw 747 banks close their doors. That is 747 named banks, keep in mind some of the banks had hundreds of branches! The start of that problem was a combination of your initial individual mortgages and the bankers' collective and mistaken outlook for a rosy future. The interest rate you paid at that time was typically a fixed rate and over time, inflation rose till it was a higher rate than the interest borrowers were paying back to the bank. Short version; banks were losing money as the spread was suddenly reversed and they were paying more than they were receiving. Politicians fixed this problem for their banking friends by relaxing credit requirements, allowing lower spreads on the interest rates and more risky investments to be labeled as assets. There you have it, essentially, the collapse of a federally insured Ponzi scheme.

In the aftermath, the adjustable rate mortgage rose prominently to the forefront of lenders' list of tools to help eliminate the banks' problems. This protected them against rapidly rising interest rates. Credit reporting became the premier tool of verification. The adjustable rate mortgage, generally used as protection against inflation for the bank, played a large part (but certainly not the only culprit) in the next crisis in the series which was the housing crash in 2008.

With its origins at the rural General Store, credit reports became the financial industry standard for farm loans, home loans, then large purchases of all sorts, then small purchases, and now damned near everything … including in many cases today; job applications. Credit agencies today know more about us financially than we know about ourselves. And don't bother complaining, they are here to stay right next to consumerism, or perhaps because of it.

# WHAT IS A BORROWER?

Now that we know how lenders work and what they look at, and why, let's look at what a borrower is. That's easy, right? Everyone who ever owed a dollar on a credit card is a borrower. But if you look at it with this new knowledge, you may find your assumptions (or what you were taught) were incorrect here as well. Things may not be that clear here either. Again think of the car buyer, and of yourself as the car dealer. The driver needs a car and the borrower needs money. The car dealer needs to sell cars and the banker needs to sell the money. And, yes, they are selling it! The car dealer doesn't want the car coming back (except to service it with oil and tire changes), and the bank doesn't want anything but the regular payments coming in. Seem to have a lot in common, right?

**Cash is nothing more than a commodity— bought and sold like everything else.**

They are polar opposites.

Bankers as well as the car dealers both have goods to move. On the one hand automobiles, the other cash. Cash then, is nothing more than a commodity meant to be bought and sold like everything else. It is us who need to look at this in a different light as there is one fundamental little difference between the car dealer and the money lender. The car dealer diligently looks for people who need and want to buy a car. The money lender looks primarily for those that do not need to borrow to whom they will readily lend. Read it again, let it sink in.

An old banker's creed, "Never lend money to anyone who needs it." If that applied to the car dealer he would not sell many cars, but it is absolutely true of a bank. So how does the bank find somebody who doesn't need money upon which to bestow buckets of cash? Through the millennia it has always been problematic for the money lender. Those who did not need to borrow would pay it back as promised. Desperate souls on the other hand, would not. Used to be quite the gamble lending money, today there are credit ratings, but the reality is that this too is but a piece of the problem. Who then, does not need to borrow money, but borrows it anyway? What happy medium might there be? The correlation is almost amusing, and it's one of the reasons I wrote this book.

I was sitting down with my family in 1984 for Thanksgiving dinner. My wife and I were married only a few years when a sibling proclaimed they had finally fallen below the $25,000 mark on their mortgage. My mother indicated how pleased she was. Not wanting to be left out, I opined we just breached the $300,000 mark and I thought my mom was going to fall out of her chair! In 1984 a house in my area could be bought for roughly $50,000 so owing that much to her was huge. But in the eyes of a banker, my sibling was in debt and I was an ally creating income streams which they converted into assets.

There is a minor difference out there in the eyes of the lender as to the definition of exactly what debt it is, but not necessarily so in the eyes of the typical borrower. A trip to Disney on Visa is debt. A margin account for stock, as well as horse racing, is gambling. Income producing real estate is an asset. Banks dislike debt. Banks like assets. An individual wearing his or her credit as a symbol of personal pride are themselves assets. You do not need to have any earned income what-so-ever to ask for and receive a million dollar loan for a good income property if it is sound, if you have a good track record, and if you treat the banker as a personal asset manager. By the same token, you will not get enough to shine your shoes if you are arrogant, negligent, and suggest to the world at large that someone owes you something.

# TYING IT ALL TOGETHER

Back to credit ratings. From 300 to 850, pick a number.[6] A few things work together, for and against, in determining this number.[7]

First, how much you owe compared to the credit limit in the account. In other words, if your credit limit on an account is $5,000 and you owe $4,700 you will score low.

Second, if the total amount you owe on all combined accounts is too high for the comfort of the income which you earn you will score low.

Third, how long your accounts have been established. The longer the payment records the better. Lots of brand spanking new accounts are frightening to lenders.

Lastly, how many inquiries have been made to your account in a reporting period? Multiple inquiries make lenders jittery as well.

You want your score high and it is really not that hard to do. You want the lender to look at your report and have integrity, honesty, and character jump off the page at him.

So, *now* it's about you.

Peruse the recommended reading list in the appendix and fix your credit if you need to. This is the single most important thing you can do for yourself financially. Get out of debt … so you can borrow money.

Your banker is your silent partner in all you care to do. Take care of him or her and develop a picture of yourself in their eyes with your credit. Your banker is a steward, a curator of something he does not own but manages for others. Use your credit as a tool to help your banker recognize you as his or her asset, and engage this relationship in your life.

I always told my children to think about things differently than most are trained to think. I contend it is better to do something today that will pay you for the rest of your life for doing it that one time. Your credit rating is the place to begin to bring these practices to fruition and put them to work for you. You have a choice as we all do from the time we are born till the time we die. Having a deep understanding of the people you are dealing with is the key to success. I do not believe in luck, although I believe wholeheartedly in the outward appearance of luck. Preparing for a job interview by researching the company history may nudge the decision in your favor.

Addressing, correcting, and managing your financial image will readily indicate your reliability and responsibility and make you an asset to the money lenders. And being an asset in the eyes of the money lenders will take you places you never imagined.

**Being an asset in the eyes of the money lenders will take you places you never imagined.**

What we have discussed sounds a lot easier than it is if you are in the tank with your credit today. Most of us don't have the $50,000 in the bank with which to purchase a small piece of planet earth either. So what to do? We talked a lot about how much money you would have in five years starting with $50,000 based on doing a variety of things with it. Establish those goals we discussed earlier right now. Determine how much you want to have and when you want to have it. If you are working and have little debt, read Dr. Thomas J. Stanley's *The Millionaire Next Door* and *The Millionaire Mind*, you are half way there. If you are out of work and loaded to the hilt with debt, go to Dave Ramsey's website www.daveramsey.com and read it all, borrow what you can and make your first investment buying his *Baby Steps Bundle*, but don't spend the money without a solemn promise to yourself to follow his guidance out of the hole you are in. Practice what he preaches and review it regularly. It took you a long time to get into this condition, getting out is not as simple as turning a light switch.

When you are finished with Dave Ramsey's material, read Dr. Stanley's books as well. This is a mindset. You have to unlearn and relearn anew. Bad habits are hard to break, but persistence and determination can prevail. I made the mistake of asking my then newlywed wife what she'd like for her birthday over 30 years ago. She told me she'd like me to quit smoking. I pleaded for her to change her mind and ask for something real, something easy—like perhaps the moon—but she refused and so I quit. This was the single most difficult thing I have ever done and I did it by continuously making little bets with myself. If I had gone for 15 minutes without smoking I would tell myself, "Bet you can't go another five." When the minutes became days and the days were rough, I would reduce the bets to hours and do something to get my mind off it. It took 30 relentless days, but finally faded away. She had the birthday gift she wanted and I thank her for it today. Again, when you feel the urge to spend yourself into a hole going out on a little binge, don't. Make a bet with yourself instead and never take your eye off the prize. Go to the public library and check out one of the recommended reading books in the appendix. You will learn an immense amount and slowly wean yourself into a new lifestyle—painlessly.

This process is not a get-rich-quick scheme. It is a lifestyle change. It is a lasting solution to a timeless problem plaguing many, if not most of us, today. It took a long time to train the way you think, it will take a long time to rethink it. Start today. A year to reprogram your mindset, and a lifetime of financial freedom awaits.

# Endnotes

1. *Model T Forum: Forum 2011* by Dennis Halpin. "Buy a Ford and Spend the Difference" ad campaign of 1923. Retrieved from http://www.mtfca.com/discus/messages/179374/181375.html?1294322210.

2. Retrieved from: http://www.adweek.com.

3. Retrieved from: http://www.ESPN.go.com.

4. Retrieved from: http://money.howstuffworks.com/personal-finance/banking/bank1.htm.

5. Retrieved from: http://www.howstuffworks.com/fed.htm.

6. Retrieved from: http://en.wikipedia.org/wiki/Credit_score_in_the_United_States.

7. Retrieved from: http://www.myfico.com/CreditEducation/articles/.

This process is not
a get-rich-quick
scheme. It is a lifestyle
change. Start today.
A year to reprogram
your mindset, and a
lifetime of financial
freedom awaits.

CHAPTER FIVE

# Starting at Zero

The money doubling scenario in chapter three was a nice exercise, but there is one problem with all such exercises of this nature: most readers don't have the $50k we used in the examples. Most people pick up their first book on real estate investing because of one common thread—they have nothing, nada, zilch, and somehow want to change all that. If you can relate to this then the next obvious question becomes, "Where do I start?"

This book is not a get-rich-quick scheme. If that's what you want forget it, I'm not offering it. If you truly believe such a thing is even possible, you need more than I can give within these pages. That does not mean that unimaginable wealth is not conceivable, just that you'll have to work at it.

A lack of confidence is a common denominator among novice investors reading about real estate investing. Most of the authors writing on the subject are seasoned professionals and can read a seller like a book and see the outcome before the initial handshake and introductions are done. You are not there yet, but I recommend you read the books and attempt to put into practice the methods they tout. One of the books the developer in Massachusetts who enticed me to invest was *Nothing Down* by Robert Allen. I have mixed feeling about this book as the concepts are not aligned with what I have done, nor are they what I recommend. It does however, offer many anecdotes that may help develop a mindset for investing. Reading is an important step in your education, but only one of several you must take to set yourself up for success. With this in mind, you should not agree with everything you read simply because it is in print. My advice here is to never forget where you came from. I feel a lot of authors do not live the principles they preach, or perhaps they simply don't remember what it was like before they could be considered successful. The more material you read, the more you will recognize what is and is not effective, what is and is not truthful or valuable. Absorb enough material on the subject to be able to make intelligent, educated decisions about the path you alone should take. Know where to go to get the information you need and how to use it to best serve your goals.

I offer the following start-up scenarios. Read them all as there is always something to be learned, but pick the one closest to your position today. The first thing you need to do is convince yourself you are absolutely no different than the folks who are doing this every day—and that is probably the hardest point to grasp.

# START-UP SCENARIO ONE: "I'M BROKE!"

I'm anxiously waiting the biography of one of my personal favorites, Ric Edelman. As of now I do not believe one is in the works, so let me tell you a quick story. His saga begins with bad advice, borrowed furniture, a one-room apartment and being out of work, to becoming the number one certified Financial Planner in the country with syndicated radio and television shows, and the author of at least a half dozen books. Like I said, I'm waiting for the biography to come out, but I suspect this, rags-to-riches story developed because he got pissed and refused to accept defeat. Rule number one: never give up. It ain't over till the fat lady sings. I do not care if this sounds cliché, it is the absolute truth. Immigrants to America do better in this country than many of the lucky ones born here—not because of what they are given by this government, but because of their attitudes and their willingness to do whatever it takes to get ahead. If we won't do something because it is beneath us, then what right do we have to the wealth we are discussing in the first place?

Mow lawns, wash dishes, walk dogs. Can't afford a lawn mower? Make a deal to split the profits with someone who has one and doesn't use it. Bottom line, you accept defeat only when you accept defeat. I do not care what your abnormality is, there is someone out there among the six billion inhabitants of this planet who is worse off than you are and has made it further with a whole lot less. Beethoven was deaf. Jim Abbott, borne without a right hand, pitched a no-hitter for the NY Yankees. Steven Hawkins, world renowned physicist cannot move a muscle in his body. Helen Keller, Stevie Wonder, Franklin Delano Roosevelt ... and a couple million more with major impediments that could have been excuses for failure. Are you healthy? If you are, there are two points to consider: 1) you never have to look to far to find someone in a whole lot worse shape than you are, and as Ric Elderman says, 2) "broke is a condition not an affliction."

If you are in scenario one, I assume your credit score is low, you have no savings account, and in yesterday's mail you received notification of this year's rent increase. Your life in general qualifies as material for a country western song, but still, all is not lost. Go to www.daveramsey.com and commit to becoming debt free.

If you are in the hole, it can take five years to turn your life around, rid yourself of debt, and establish your position to make your first purchase. Use this time wisely and train yourself to make sound financial decisions from here on out. Be prolific with your reading and your associations. Save every dime you can save and eliminate every penny of debt without damaging your credit any further. Move in with mom and dad or share a place with a friend, sell the Mercedes and buy a used bicycle.

**Consider every action against the goal you create.**

The single toughest thing I ever did was give my wife the birthday present she wanted—for me to quit smoking. The principals here are exactly the same. Keep the goal on the absolute forefront of your mind. Consider every action against the goal you create. Never blink. If your friends, family and associates are not supportive, find new friends and associates. Sorry you're stuck with family, but you can use them as a challenge to turn their way of thinking to match yours. Whoever said you have to be the weak one in the group?

# START-UP SCENARIO TWO: "I LIVE PAYCHECK TO PAYCHECK"

The second scenario we will cover is for those fortunate individuals who already have jobs and are meeting their monthly bills, but who have little to no savings or other resources. They might be tenants living under the control of landlords or with parents and so-on.

If you are in this category my top recommendation is to buy Dr. Thomas J. Stanley's *The Millionaire Next Door*. This is required reading for anyone in scenario two. This book is a smart, thought-provoking and intuitive observation that will never be outdated. Read it more than once. Practice what he preaches. Look around your own neighborhood, and observe firsthand how utterly correct he is and perhaps, see a bit of insight into yourself as to how limited you see those around you. To see different things, learn to look from different perspectives.

While you are doing this, continue to build your Dave Ramsey savings account and once you have your first $1,000 in the bank, do something else as well, something outside of the "Dave Ramsey Doctrine." Use that savings account (what Ramsey calls your "Emergency Fund") as collateral for a personal loan from the same bank that has the savings account. Borrow $1,000.00 from the bank and deposit those funds into that same account. Make the payments dutifully every month till paid in full and then do it again. Build yourself a credit history at the same time you begin building your savings account. While you are getting out of debt you are learning all there is to know about financing and investing. It is not counter-intuitive to do this even though you will be going against the grain of what you are learning through Dave Ramsey's process.

Ramsey's program is designed to get you out of debt, permanently—a situation not conducive to building wealth through real estate investing. Dr. Stanley's objective is to make you recognize those habits that got you into debt and ultimately make you select better choices. These are very good goals to have, both of which you should strictly adhere to, but remember my goal is to get you out of debt and free of financial bondage so you can invest in real estate!

This then comes down to having the right mental attitude. You need to develop this mental attitude for two reasons. First, the end game is to become financially independent, but in order to do that you need to think like the financially independent person you are trying to become and financially independent people do not think the way most everyday blue collar people think. Not even close. Secondly, money itself will not make a person wealthy. Attitude about money will. Money will flow towards the person with the proper attitude as readily as it will be repelled by the person with an indifferent outlook. Not at all unlike the appearance of luck coming to the prepared. Clip a coupon, recycle the cans and bottles and put the money in the savings account, make the coffee at home and brown bag it to lunch. This alone will get you the savings account you'll need. One of my favorite financial philosophies comes from Ric Edelman, "It's not about how much you make; it's about how much you keep." His book *The Truth About Money* is another excellent reference for how to start saving from within the confines of your existing lifestyle. This book should be one of the first in everybody's personal financial library as a well-worn reference tool!

## START-UP SCENARIO THREE: "I'M READY FOR FINANCIAL INDEPENDENCE"

This brings us to our third consideration, those who are working, have some savings, but are just a little concerned about their long-term financial future, people who know that's not all there is. For those of you in this category, I state simply, keep reading. You are positioned to begin more quickly than people in the first two scenarios. Your challenge is to make the right moves from the beginning.

Whether you have a lot of work to do to get your financial house in order or you have only to make a few minor adjustments to your attitude towards investing before your journey to financial independence begins, the rest of this book is dedicated to making that happen. As you continue reading, you will learn a great deal about investigating, selecting, buying and ultimately, managing property. I will speak to each of these categories and provide the chronological order that steps should naturally occur. Let's begin with what it means to manage property and if you should even be a landlord.

# Part II

## M I N D S E T

You can delegate authority, not responsibility. Before deciding to open your own business or before buying investment real estate, you must first and foremost be capable and willing of accepting responsibility for your own actions. At the closing table, there will be a tremendous amount of paperwork. One paper you will not find at that table, however, is a disclosure statement exonerating you from sole responsibility—there will not be anyone left to blame.

If you make a sound and profitable investment there is no requirement to share your success. Likewise, nobody will be taking the blame should you make a bad investment.

CHAPTER SIX

# What Are You
# Really Renting?

Before we look at what is entailed in purchasing, owning, and managing rental income property, it is hugely important to understand what personal commitment will be required from you, the potential owner. It is not like cash, bonds, or stock—buy and forget does not apply. It requires time, patience, and a strong psychological outlook steeped in determination. Such an endeavor cannot be equated with any of the passive investment comparisons we used earlier, nor can we link the concept of creating rental income to owning a business. Though managing rental properties includes more aspects of business ownership than other investment options, this is the closest you can come to owning your own business while still allowing you to work full-time at a primary job. It will produce handsome passive income if done correctly. Your outlook is most important and from that perspective you must understand and believe beyond the shadow of a doubt that:

- This IS a business.

- It is YOUR BUSINESS.

- TENANTS are your CUSTOMERS.

What exactly does it mean to "manage" property? I suspect many who enter the property owner and management business believe it to be as simple as collect rent, pay the mortgage, and enjoy the difference as passive income. If you believe this to be true, then I suppose you might also believe that spending a week as a fast food fry cook would qualify you to teach at the Culinary Institute.

So after you research, analyze, and purchase your first rental income property, you become a landlord and as such you will embark on renting your first apartment. You'll put ads in newspapers and on-line, and reach out to realtors to find the perfect match for your apartment.

Well, sort of. This may sound funny, but what you are technically looking to fill is not just space but, space-time. Albert Einstein would be proud. Here's why. You can never receive an income from a unit for the time it is not inhabited—obvious, right? If a tenant vacates in July and the unit is not occupied until September when a new tenant moves in, you cannot tell these new tenants they need to pay you for the month of August because if they don't you will lose money. Not only won't they care, they'll think you're certifiably insane for asking. Mathematically it looks like this.

Say you have a thousand dollar a month apartment with a one year lease, and at the end of the year you raise the rent 5%. The tenant gets pissed off and leaves. You don't just lose the $50.00 increase ($1,000 x 5% = $50.00), you likely lose the $1,000 you would have received for the original rental amount collected from your happy tenant. On top of that the cost of advertising and repair costs associated with getting the place ready for a new tenant. If this is what happens, and you fill the vacancy after only one month you start with a vacancy factor above 8%, (1 month vacant divided by 12 months in a year = 8%) plus costs. You may find yourself out of pocket by as much as $1,750 when adding together lost rent, advertising, carpet cleaning, and repainting. That equates to 15% of the annual income for that apartment! ($1,000 per month x 12 months = $12,000 annual rent. $1,750 combined loss and outflow divided by $12,000 = 15%) This is a typical scenario that started with you raising the rent on an apartment because you bought an apartment building to make money and the tenants thought you were greedy and left. Sounds like a vicious circle doesn't it? I could easily get into cliché central here, but will spare you through respect for your intelligence. Here's the short version.

You are never going to make any money in real estate if the only thing you care about is the money you make from real estate.

You make your money from your tenants. Happy tenants. Unhappy tenants will not be tenants for long. Unhappy tenants will cause you vacancies. Vacancies lose you money. Tenants, therefore, are your profit margins' best friend. They are the customers you need to satisfy and therefore create loyalty. Consider where you would be without them. All tenant problems—regardless of how trivial—are your problem. (See Table 1.8.) Later on in this chapter we will discuss how to raise rents and have the tenants say they are sorry for making you have to do it!

> **You are never going to make any money in real estate if the only thing you care about is the money you make from real estate.**

When you leave the closing table as a proud building owner, you will not just have bought a building; you will have begun a career in a service industry. We all tend to get irate when we think we should be the center of attention and for whatever reason, are not. Imagine you are engaged in an important, life-changing conversation with a person that suddenly decides to answer a text. This is not going to leave a good impression. Nor will their acting disinterested, detached, nonchalant, or like we are simply wasting their time.

Let's go back to the beginning, shall we? You've researched, analyzed and purchased your first rental income property. You are a new landlord and about to embark on the task of *keeping* your first *tenant*. Notice the subtle differences.

# THE TENANT'S VIEW

In this business I strive to keep all tenants long term. There are several important factors in keeping tenants in an apartment for the long term, but first allow me to define "long term" as those tenancies which exceed seven years. I very much like these tenants. A one month vacancy every seven years relates to a vacancy factor of just over 1%. (7 years x 12 months = 84 months. 1 / 84 = 1.19%) The vacancy you did not incur each year was money to spend. We will discuss more about vacancy factors in the next chapters.

The first and foremost concern of keeping tenants this long is to ensure they stay happy with the place they are in. Lifestyles change, families grow, jobs relocate—in short, life gets in the way of plans. There will always be reasons for people to want to move or have to move. You however, should never be one of those reasons! Equipment will fail, ovens die, toilets back up, and roofs leak. Take care of these when they happen. Don't make a tenant call you six times. You have to get it in your head you are here to serve them! Treat them the way you would want to be treated if you were a tenant. It really is that simple.

Many people cringe at the mention of toilets backing up, but the truth of the matter is it happens no more frequently in an apartment than it does in your own home. And, when I say to "take care of them when they happen," if you really don't like that sort of thing, have the phone number of a plumber on hand. Your task when receiving a phone call from a tenant is as simple as making a phone call to a plumber. I have a particular philosophical mindset with my tenants and I reiterate it to them whenever the situation allows. If someone asks about painting the place and changing the color I will tell them this: "You may paint the place purple with big green spots if that's what you like, so long as when you leave you put it back the way it was when you moved in." It usually gets a chuckle, and I've yet to run across anyone that extreme, but it does something else of much greater importance. First, it demonstrates you care: human to human as opposed to landlord to tenant. Secondly, it communicates dignity and respect when I follow up saying, "This is your home. It is my house, but it is your home first. I expect you to be able to live your life as you see fit so long as the style you choose does not adversely affect the other tenants in the building and is within the laws that govern this village and state."

I have found this to be hugely effective in tearing down preconceived psychological barriers. It provides an approachable personality, a pleasant alternative of an all too common preselected perception between a tenant and the "lord" of the land.

Allow me to give a beautiful explanation of this philosophy in a dissimilar setting using a conversation I had with a government bureaucracy.

I had purchased a parcel of land with some wetlands on it and had heard war stories of people getting into trouble with the DEC (Dept. of Environmental Conservation) after doing things they were not allowed to do. So I called the DEC myself. After getting one of the law enforcement officers on the phone I asked what I was allowed to do on my wetlands, and she asked what I had planned to do. I told her really, nothing, but was just curious. She replied that I needed to give her a possible scenario to work with and I said, "Perhaps I will build a two acre pond." I will never forget her response: "Anything you would do that would be detrimental to our wetlands we would review very unfavorably." No hesitation, no compunction, simply put, ouch! I thought that was quite extreme but for whatever reason I held my tongue and asked, "Okay, how about a gazebo or hiking paths?" Her response was just a wee bit different this time: "Anything you would do that would enhance your ability to enjoy your wetlands we would review very favorably." No hesitation, no compunction, but abundant clarity. Read both of those again. In one situation I would have the fight of my life on my hands. In the other, they would help me in any way they could.

You can deal with a hundred different government agencies and never get as clear an answer as I did with that question. Our picture of government agencies is nothing but red tape and brick walls. It is a stereotype firmly established in our minds. Never dealing with remotely close to the same number of landlords as government agents, a tenant will stereotype landlords after having dealt with only two or three, and sometimes just one.

It takes a long time for a tenant with one bad landlord to trust another. On the same hand, a tenant who learns (or just suspects) you are not trustworthy, are greedy, or whatever else they may think, will take a very long time to change their opinion of you—if ever. Many folks who have lived in small residential buildings have been treated poorly by their landlords. I know this because the reasons they are usually seeking new apartments are often the same … and I always ask! Their calls for service are ignored, but if the rent is late they are served immediate notice. They are asked if they really need that faucet fixed, but are always expected to pay late fees and interest. They are told they have to buy the paint if they want to paint the place after four years of tenancy. The driveway is never plowed, the lawn is mowed monthly and looks like an unruly wild meadow, the roof leaks, and instead of the landlord fixing it they are asked to put a bucket under it.

Tenants who call with a dripping faucet should expect to have that drip taken care of without having to call again. Set an appointment at the time they call and keep the appointment. If they leave a message, call them back, set and then keep the appointment. Analyze rents in your market continuously and let them know they will not be getting an increase this year since they have been doing a great job keeping costs down. I have even *lowered* tenants' rents when the market has taken a down turn or when they have fallen on hard times. I have waived the late fees and allowed them to pay their rent incrementally at times. You have to be very careful here and never allow them to think they are in control. Be compassionate, but firm. Be human with understanding, but with businesslike demeanor. Be consistent. Into every life a little rain will fall, and your attitude to their situation will have the ability to define their rain as either a drizzle or a deluge. Their attitude of you for how you handle their situation may mark the difference between a 1% vacancy factor and a 15% cost factor. It really does pay to be nice. Take notice of their needs and desires and simply treat your tenants as though they are actual human beings. By the way, for a tenant to have a late fee forgiven will only be considered if they make contact with me. No tenant I have to track down will ever be rewarded with a break. This is the "businesslike demeanor" just mentioned.

# YOUR REVENUE RESOURCE

Every business plan addresses sources of revenue and rentals are your business. From this perspective, tenants are your revenue source. Repetition is your value proposition. They work in concert with one another. The difference between a 15% and 1% per annual cost structure really does come down to how you treat and interact with the tenants in your building. It takes time, patience, and practice to get it right. But getting it right is directly transformed into profits. Getting it right will undoubtedly keep your tenants longer, though you will never reach a zero vacancy factor.

Let's say you have done everything right and still have a vacancy to fill. You placed a professionally printed sign in the window, on the lawn, and on the site down the road where all the political signs sprout each election year. You ran an ad in the local paper, placed photos on Craigslist™ and local sites, spread the news by word of mouth to friends and family and, finally, your phone rings ... now what?

Most of my screening is prescreening and happens right at the initial phone call. The conversation usually sounds something like this: "Hi. I'm Katherine and I'm calling about the two-bedroom apartment." If it has been rented you would stop at this point and tell her it is no longer available. If it is open I reassure the caller and state, "It is still available" and follow up with, "what can I tell you about it?" This allows them to ask what is important to them and for you to steer the conversation that follows. It is illegal to refuse to rent to a person because of their race, religion, age, sex, etc. It is not illegal to tell an exotic dancer you will not rent an apartment in a family orientated building. You do not have to accept dogs, or social services applicants. If you have a two-bedroom apartment and the bedroom is small you have the right to tell them you are limiting the occupancy to two adults and one child.

These are all things I want to know before I make an appointment to show the unit and I find out by asking who the apartment is for. I make light of it such as; "Is this for yourself, married, kids, dogs, horses?" After telling me of their situation, more often than not I will suggest the apartment they are calling about will not meet their needs and politely decline to show it. I have had people call on ads for two bedroom apartments with four children. I flat out refuse to entertain such nonsense. You will not have enough in your maintenance budget line to account for the "normal wear and tear" that will be done in these situations. Do not allow these things to occur. Set the standards and stick to them.

> **Set the standards and stick to them.**

Why is this important? Because you are after a long term relationship with a tenant, not a quick fix to fill a vacancy. Just because an applicant has a handful of cash for the security deposit and this month's rent does not mean they can pay the rent next month. Architectural problems with sound proofing are amplified when a building with two young families has a new tenant move into the vacant apartment next door consisting of two young single female bartenders from the biker club down the road. Three older couples won't mix well with a single parent of three preschoolers and a pair of beagles. You have to know the blend of the population and work towards maintaining the harmony within. And, you have to do this within the legal parameters that govern discrimination. I have always found that religious and racial mixes do not matter one iota in a building composition. They will all get along just fine because of their other commonalities, but dope smoking teenagers in a building with seniors or preschoolers will empty that building in short order.

Assuming I don't disqualify the caller immediately, I will set up an appointment to show the apartment as soon as physically possible. Prospective tenants responding to your ad are shopping for an apartment and either want or need to move. If they were interested in your ad enough to call you, they probably called in response to several other ads as well. People are somewhat impatient. If you tell them you can show it now and they accept, take it. If you tell them you can show in four days, chances are they will have either forgotten the appointment or will have already signed a lease with the competition across the street. Prompt action often creates a favorable result.

Meet the tenants in the street if possible and walk them into the building pointing things out along the way. I use this time for small talk as well and usually ask if they have looked at many places. If they tell me yes, I'll ask what the competition looks like out there. This often generates interesting conversation and it confirms my suspicions of the majority of non-professional or "accidental" landlords—landlords by default through inheritance or with dreams of a quick real estate empire.

After showing the apartment, I ask directly if they are interested in the place. If they are I ask them to fill out an application. If they are not, I ask what they would have preferred seeing and what the specific reasons this apartment does not meet their expectation. The answers actually help me see things I may have overlooked previously and can offer to fix. In my experience, sincerity can cause the prospects to call again in a couple of days.

If they are interested in the apartment I hand them the application and a pen and let them know I need it filled out now. It is not an application to take home and mail in. I do this because when they hand it back I review it in front of them and ask any clarifying questions and make notes of their answers directly on the page and line in question. This gives me a huge advantage because I ask them the question and peer directly into their eyes as they answer. Eye contact is huge. If they have a hard time making or keeping this contact or get flustered or red faced or any combination of a thousand of other little nuances, I make note of these things as well. It may not be that they are outright lying to you, they may simply not know. But if the question is "How much do you earn?" and on that line the husband writes $60k, I will ask "Sixty thousand a year?" I will watch his wife's reaction. These are sometimes very amusing. Again I won't consider them to be outright liars, but I will annotate odd reactions by asterisks and such and ask for collaborating evidence later such as tax returns, pay statements, and the like.

By far the four most important questions on my applications are as follows:

- Why are you moving?
- Have you ever broken a lease?
- Have you ever been sued in a court of law for non-payment?
- Have you ever been convicted of a felony?

Only a positive answer to the last question will cause the applicant to lose an apartment in any building I own. The other questions are there for me to generate a verbal exchange. I cannot begin to state the number of times I have heard war stories beginning with "My landlord is a #$%@... idiot!" I love these people! I have rented to tenants who have been sued by landlords when they failed to pay rent after the landlord ignored their complaints and they knew of no other recourse to get his attention. I have rented to tenants who have sued their landlords for failing to return security deposits. The question regarding "Why are you moving?" generates more personal insight than any other question I could possibly ask. I listen to the answer for context, let them ramble on.

Sometimes people simply move because they need a bigger place—great, but nowhere near as entertaining. (I love a good story!)

Sometimes however, the problem is not with the landlord, but the tenant. That will come out as well. Important telltale signs of problems inevitably show up during the conversations over the application and the tour, sometimes with enough conviction to deny the apartment on the spot. However, I will never tell a prospective tenant they either do, or do not have an agreement at the time they fill out the application. Nor do I ever allow an applicant to move in without an application. I always tell them it will take at least a couple of days to check their references, even if I have made up my mind on the spot one way or the other. I never tell them my decision at the time they initially see the apartment. I have no problem what-so-ever telling any prospective tenant they were not selected for an apartment, and if they ask why I generally tell them I simply selected a more qualified applicant.

Do not be fooled by the color of money. Allowing an unworthy tenant can be costly in dollars and time, and can be psychologically draining. It is almost always avoidable. I have had a total of three full evictions in my thirty years in this business. Two of these were tenants

I received as a part of the purchase of a property. The other was a tenant I did not interview. I was away on business and delegated the task. I attribute this success entirely to my selection process and my follow-up interaction with them as their landlord.

Upon completing the application and securing all necessary signatures, I walk them out of the building to answer any last minute questions, tell them when I will get back to them and the like, but the *real* reason is to get a look at the condition of the car they arrived in. An old beat up band-aid stickered car is not the concern, but a heaping pile of fetid trash on the floorboards is. You can rest assured the way they keep their car is the same way they will keep your house. You often have but 15 - 30 minutes to read these applicants. You need to get it right. If you are not sure about something in particular, call and ask for clarification.

> The way a prospective tenant keeps their car is the same way they will keep your house.

I usually tell the prospect I will get back to them in no more than three days. During this three day period I do a couple of things. I sometimes drive by the address they put down as current address and take a quick look. I call the references they list and inquire about their character (though I do not put a lot of emphasis on the answers I get). I analyze their income to debt as listed on their application to get a feel for whether they can actually afford to pay the rent. I have called young couples just starting out in life and told them they could have the apartment if they can arrange a co-signer for the lease. Before I bother to do this, however, everything else will have had to have checked out.

One of the other important considerations for me is their relationship with their present landlord. This was discussed in the negative previously, but there is another side that is equally as important. Not all landlords are trolls. They really might need a bigger place. Your prospective tenant may very well love their current landlord, this also happens frequently, you just don't see them as often since content tenants are not typically shopping for apartments. The question then is how long do they stay under each roof and what trends are showing there. Four places in four years is not a hot prospect to me.

On the flip side of analyzing prospects is the credit report. Personally, I don't use them. Many landlords I know use them emphatically. My opinion here is there is way too much emphasis waged on this bet. Everything I do is on a personal level, eye contact, reactions from spouses to answers, the look and care for the car, the discipline of the kids while the parents are looking and filling out the application etc. Credit reports are for corporate entities, large complexes where management and ownership are not one in the same. Those entities removed from any personal interactions where there simply are no other options available. I trust my instincts and will work with the tenants to keep them in the building when things get a little less than perfect in their lives—as happens in all our lives. Credit reports simply don't allow a human side to be reflected in the equation. If I were selling a house and holding a mortgage, I need the credit report. It is a far less effective measuring stick for filling vacancies.

## WHEN YOU MUST RAISE RENT

Keeping tenants in excess of 7 years does not mean you keep the rents the same as the day they moved in. However, you can raise rent in a systematic fashion and with full disclosure that involves them in the process. Water bills rise as do taxes, insurance, maintenance fees, etc.

The following is an excerpt from a letter I presented to a tenant a few years ago.

Dear _____,

As you know, in the past I have been able to hold off rent adjustments to your apartment, absorbing escalations in water and garbage removal as well as tax increases and rising costs in other areas. If you have been paying attention to the current state of affairs in both City and State governments, you know the issue with rising taxes is only part of a much larger picture. There are multiple factors at work against us this year which I simply cannot absorb and must therefore make a rent adjustment. Here is a list of factors affecting this decision:

- Tax increase of 71% this year (305% over 3 years)
- Water rate increase of 45%
- Garbage collection increase of 33%
- Insurance increase of 59%

I apologize, but I am sure you can see how these changes are not sustainable for me to absorb at the current rate of rent and I'm afraid I have no choice but to pass a portion of these increases down.

The rent for the apartment you are residing in will increase $100 (from your current rate of $700/month to the new rate of $800/month). This change will be effective beginning __/__/____, I know this is difficult and requires an adjustment in your budget as well, believe me it is not something I wanted to do. Our history together I think, speaks clearly in that regard. Currently you are one of my longest term tenants and I sincerely hope this remains the case.

Regrettably,

Bob Pritchard

Consider that there are several "taxes" which together comprise "real estate tax." The letter does not state that <u>all</u> taxes went up 71%. Nor do the notes regarding water, garbage, or insurance state that those increases all occurred within the past calendar year. These increases have been emphasized (selectively) to get the point across clearly to the tenant. My costs go up, yours do too.

As long as your rents do not climb dramatically above the local area average, it is doubtful there will be challenges to your increase. I cannot stress enough how important it is to keep your rental rates on par with area averages. An explanation of why this is critical will be provided in later chapters.

I did not mail this letter to my tenant, I hand delivered it personally, as I almost always do. The personal approach keeps you connected <u>with</u> your tenant instead of <u>over</u> them. Just taking the time to be involved and being there in person to hear their pain pays huge dividends in loyalty and understanding. On my way out, these tenants assured me they would be more careful in the use of the water so that I would not have to "go through this again." This was a few years ago and these same tenants have since been notified that their rent will, "most probably go up $200/month within the next few months." This softens the blow and gives them time to prepare.

Everybody expects rent increases. How you do it makes the difference on how it is received and responded to. Very early in my career, I lived that difference between a 15% cost and a 1% vacancy. You would be very wise to adopt the personal approach and create understanding rather than repeating my costly mistake.

Treat your tenants
the same way you
would want to
be treated if you
were a tenant, and
the relationship
will prosper.

CHAPTER SEVEN

# On Becoming a Respected Landlord

Respect is something a lot of people believe comes with position, but respect is elusive for many. Newly appointed supervisors often make the mistake of thinking that their position comes with a certain level of automatic respect. The military demands respect for positions of power, but the people in the positions do not always warrant the respect the position mandates. As an employer, a supervisor, or even a military member, your job is to ensure the task at hand is completed correctly and in a timely manner. Your employees work for you, but (and herein lies a lot of the misconstrued notion), you work for your employees. Likewise, your tenants generate income for you. But you have to work for them to keep them content in order to ensure they continue to generate that income.

As a supervisor at your job, it may be your responsibility to see schedules are executed on time and shortfalls are filled. You may have to make whatever adjustments might be necessary to keep whatever you manage running smoothly. It is also your job to see that employees have the tools, training, and support they need to complete the bidding you require of them. It is a two way street. They work for you, but you also work for them. Their needs are your responsibility to fill so that they are able to meet your needs in production. How well you balance these two sides will indicate the level of respect you will generate. Working for a bad boss causes people to start perusing the job market and wears out the copier with resumes.

Being a landlord is no different. Tenants with uncaring landlords start apartment shopping. Moving is not fun for anyone and nobody enjoys it. Preventing tenants from feeling as though they need to move should be easier to overcome than making them want to move. Be the landlord your tenants are looking for.

During an initial interview with a prospective tenant I make it very clear that I own the building, and that is exactly how I refer to it—as an inanimate object, but suggesting pride of ownership and responsibility in management. I also make it clear that this building is an excellent place for them to make their "home"—suggesting personal engagement and fulfillment. The first encounter they have of me keeping my word to them is when I follow up as promised about whether or not I am accepting them as tenants. I write down the time and date I plan to respond and make sure this is when I call them. If I forget, the only thing they will remember is that I did not keep my word. No excuse will matter. Mutual respect begins right there.

With the risk of sounding flippant, the rest is really quite easy. You have an obligation to the bank, the assessor, the insurance company, the lawn maintenance crew, etc. Tenants have an obligation to you for the rent and reimbursement of any bills paid by you on their behalf. If they call you with a hot water problem or a leaking faucet, fix it. Call whoever is necessary and get it taken care of immediately. Later when they are late with the rent, remind them the service they receive from you is no different from the service you expect to receive from them. I have had tenants behind on their rent call with problems and I address the issues in the same immediate manner as though they were not behind with their rent. The argument of your actions is compelling and embarrassing for them when you do ask for the rent. I am not against subtly reminding tenants who are a little behind on their rent that my service to them appears to be a higher priority than their obligation to me, but I will not discuss their late rent as I am fixing their faucet. I will bank it for when I come to call upon them.

This little difference is as important as it is difficult to accomplish. If a tenant is behind in the rent, or in fulfilling any other obligation to you, there is a natural tendency to hold one (the late rent) hostage against the other (the leaky faucet) and this is exactly where the mutual respect deteriorates. The two problems are not related. Keeping them separate is your problem.

Most times what happens is a guilt trip. The tenant has to call you to get the faucet fixed but will be reluctant to do so because they "know" you will be yelling about the rent in arrears. Assuming they sheepishly call anyway—and the exchange between you has no mention of the late rent, they are surprised and elated. This should be even more reinforced when you come and fix the faucet without mentioning the rent in arrears except on your way out the door as a simple reminder that you will "see them on Thursday" for the balance of the rent "as they promised" during your last conversation. If you are successfully able to keep these two distinctly different issues separate and still focus exclusively on their problem, their respect for you will automatically increase. You have begun the path of building a team with your tenant for the mutual benefit of both.

> **You and your tenants are a team. There is mutual benefit for both.**

There are tenants who never miss or are delayed on their obligations to you and these folks are great, but most are human and humans are not perfect. They are not perfect in your eyes, and you are not perfect in theirs. Mutual respect is a process, not a rite of passage emanating from your attendance at the closing table as a buyer.

I once had a tenant fall two weeks behind in their rent after boasting about the beautiful seven day cruise they had just returned from. Though this happened some time ago, it still tops the list of requiring the most personal restraint on my part. I did a great job of biting my tongue as they described in detail the ports of call and excursions and balconied room all paid for with the help of my money! But I did. I was able to express my happiness with their vacation and we exchanged nothing but pleasantries during the entire conversation. At the end as the conversation came around to the rent, it was my turn to let them know about the $3.00 per day late fees and that my expectation was as they had told me—that I would be able to pick up the rent from them on the 18th of the month. I could have blown up or created an unpleasant moment that might have remained associated with me every time they thought about their cruise. I didn't. Instead, on the 18th, I picked up the rent along a $54.00 bonus for my patience.

My number one path to generate respect through the eyes of any tenant is a continuous display of respect from me for that tenant.

I tell all new tenants the same thing every time one moves into one of my apartments, *"My desire is for you to live your life as you see fit, so long as that style does not adversely affect the other tenants in this building. Likewise I expect them to be able live their lives as they see fit so long as that lifestyle does not adversely affect yours."*

# CLEAR COMMUNICATION

One of the biggest keys to keeping balanced harmony is clear communication. Clear concise verbal and written communication is only one part, the other is the intentional and or unintentional communication your actions make on your behalf. Much of this nonverbal communication just happens and we only hear of it though rumors, by what others say about us.

People are people. So are you and I. It stands to reason that our lives then are no more or less perfect than the lives of our tenants. We make mistakes, have bad days, and every once in a while we simply wish everyone would just go away. If we have a bad day, little things make it worse. That aside, there are two simple rules that apply to you in terms of dealing with your tenants:

- Don't display the notion you are better than they are.
- Never display the notion you are better off than they are.

Don't display the notion you are better than they are first and foremost, because you are not. The best way to keep yourself on the same plane as your tenants is to simply respect them. Listen to them, converse with them, and be friendly with them. Actively engage when they tell you of their vacation down to the beach last weekend, smile at the photos of their grandkids and be sincere when they tell the woes of the transmission failing. In short, be a human being.

You have a life as well as a lifestyle no different than your tenants do. Yours is no better than theirs or worse. It's just different. If you just bought a brand new 28' cabin cruiser, don't show them pictures and tell them they paid for it, don't take their parking spot for your wintering storage ground or tell them their rent is going to go up because you didn't realize how much gas the damn thing burns. Don't collect rent in your brand new "E" Class Mercedes and don't pull out a wad of bills that could choke a horse to make change for their measly rent. Simple respect is the key to harmonious relationships between tenants and landlords, and the key to getting it right is to not forget where you came from. Check your ego and your pride.

Verbal communication outside of idle chit-chat is important. Most important is the listening portion. You need to know what is said or told to you and you cannot do that by putting yourself on a pedestal. Still there are times when it must be made clear where you stand in the grand scheme of things. Sometimes absolutely clear, firm, and precise communication is necessary. When required it needs to be done expeditiously. During these times the manner of your delivery as well as the message can be elevated as a reminder of the "This is my house …" portion of the rules. Make it clear what your expectations are, but maintain a polite and compassionate demeanor.

I recently had an interesting problem with a tenant's underage child having a drinking party in the backyard of one of my buildings with a small group of his friends. The police were called by a neighbor and arrests were made. One of the older tenants in the building was also allegedly present during the party, but had retired for the evening prior to the police arrival. The parents of the child were never notified by the police of the arrest since the child was arrested as an adult and there was no technical need to do so. I found out about the incident by police officers involved in the case, most of whom are friends of mine.

As landlord you have an obligation for the safety of the tenants in your building; all of them. There are many building owners that would have simply said, "The police are handling it." But this is wrong and there were multiple things to address.

Upon hearing of police action, I knocked on the tenant's door to find out firsthand what had transpired. I quickly learned that I was the bad guy telling these tenants their son and his friends were arrested for drinking and possession of marijuana. Upon seeing the exasperated looks on their face, I told them I would get back to them with the facts of the case in greater detail.

Since the parents had no knowledge of the incident at all, I interviewed the arresting officer, read the police report, and spoke personally with the Chief of Police and drafted the following letter to ensure all they never forget whose building this is:

> According to the police report covering the arrest of your son, _____ on_____ you are in technical default of the terms of the lease you signed.
>
> This shall serve as a clear warning that any further illegal activities on/in these premises shall result in immediate termination of your lease through proper legal channels.
>
> I think you and I have been associated long enough for you to know I am a man of my word.
>
> You have a situation on your hands upon which you need to get control. Your failure to take control of this situation will cause me to have to take control for you.
>
> I assure you my methodology of handling this situation will be much more uncomfortable than were you to handle it personally. Regardless, it will be remedied.
>
> Your lease is based on a thirty-day agreement and can be canceled at any time by both yourself and by myself without cause. Do not make a bad situation worse. I will not see this property become a haven for wandering strays bringing undue attention upon themselves when they are misguided and lacking direction.
>
> Your total and immediate attention is required. Do not allow this activity to be repeated on my property. Failure to comply will result in termination of your lease."

The "older" individual who was allegedly involved was the live-in boyfriend of the tenant whose name was on the lease. Technically therefore, he was not a tenant, but rather a guest of the tenant. The lease stated two adults and one child without naming the individual. I typed the following letter and presented it to all of the tenants in the building which was equally as stern stating;

> According to the terms of the leases signed by all tenants of the above property the agreement to lease the property is between the signatory names on the lease and landlord only.
>
> All signatory lease holders shall be held accountable for the actions of their guests and children as well as the guests of those children.
>
> According to the terms of the lease, "Tenant shall comply with all statutes, ordinances and requirements of all municipal, state and federal authorities now in force or which may hereinafter be in force pertaining to the use of the premises." Failure to comply could be considered a breach of contract. Breach of contract is grounds for default. Default is grounds for removal.
>
> Signatory tenants who knowingly and/or willfully permit illegal activities to occur on the premises will be immediately removed from the premises through legal means.
>
> I want to make this perfectly clear that this building is a family oriented building which I strive to maintain for the safe and harmonious use and I will not tolerate the well-being of any tenant to be in jeopardy by the illegal activities of another, their children or their guests."

This letter was signed and distributed to all remaining tenants in the building for three purposes. First, to assuage the uncomfortable feelings of the innocent tenants in the building that I didn't care or know what is going on. Second, it served as a warning shot across the bow to the tenant who escaped the clutches of the police that this was not acceptable behavior and that I knew all about it. Lastly, to let all the tenants know I am not afraid to take necessary action to protect their homes.

One letter, three meanings, immediate and clear response and their respect for me increased as they all very clearly understood once again: I am a man of my word and I expect nothing less in return.

At the same time this was taking place, the notion of tact and diplomacy was prevalent. There was no guesswork except on the notion that the parents were never informed by the police. I had no rational expectation that the parents would not have been informed, but they were not. The kids were all released on their own recognizance. Go figure. There was no rebuttal by any tenant on the facts surrounding this, there was no guessing as to where I stood in the situation—none. Most importantly, there was no yelling, no finger pointing, and no false accusations. All the tenants remained in good standing and there were no repeat offenses.

This scenario had a tendency to frighten a couple of the folks who were close to it at the time. I was told by an officer that they would handle the situation and that I should not get involved. While I appreciate their motive, and understand that past experiences for them may have included anger or instability from a landlord, for my personal style of tenant involvement, staying clear of the incident would have been the wrong choice. You can delegate authority, but not responsibility. As a landlord you are responsible for the safety and wellbeing of your tenants. Had I not gotten involved, the remaining tenants would have grown concerned by my inaction and since all charges were dropped, the lack of any message would have been construed

> You can delegate authority, but not responsibility.

as permission to proceed and that such action were deemed to be acceptable. As for time, it took me no more than an hour to word the letters. I delivered them personally and read the first to the tenants of the child in question and the second to the tenant who escaped the clutches of the police. Two and a half hours total time spent. Permanent solution installed and no equivocation on mutual understanding.

CHAPTER EIGHT

# Dealing with Occasional Problems

As a landlord, problems will inevitably creep into your life. Becoming a respected landlord can minimize the impact of these events, but people are people. None of us are perfect and life gets in the way of plans.

When you have to take action, I have found the only effective approach is immediate, forceful and with resolve.

Solvable situations—noise, hot water heater keeps going out, arrest for underage drinking by a bunch of one tenant's guests, and unruly kids are all easy. Some other problems are not.

Problems are often not as they first appear. The worst nightmares of a tenant are not the same worst nightmares of the owner. If you want tenants to stay in your building, the key is you must see the problems and concerns of the tenants through the eyes of the tenant and not through your eyes as a landlord.

With that said, tenants' problems do not necessarily have to become your problems, but tenants need to know you are there for them and not just the rent check. It is entirely possible to elevate your position in the eyes of a tenant and consequently, your personal finances simply by knowing the rules of engagement and helping solve the dilemmas your tenants get themselves into on occasion. Knowing who to call and helping tenants make those calls can literally make the difference between a costly eviction (and consequent remodel) and keeping a tenant for a very long time. Sometimes it is as easy as accepting a short delay in receiving the rent. Sometimes making a call on a tenant's behalf or filling out assistance paperwork such as landlord statements is all it takes. I've directed tenants to employers, given character references and placed calls to people I know looking to hire with recommendations. Keep in mind your own reputation is at stake so they have to be worthy first! But, as helping them helps you, spending an hour assisting a tenant down on their luck can be extremely valuable investment of your time. When successful, it warms the heart.

> A short delay in receiving rent may have long term payoff.

For instance, I once had a tenant who decided she absolutely could not get along with her boss and quit her job as sole breadwinner, and gave up her health insurance, knowing she had a son with asthma at home. She quit, had no unemployment, no prospects, and seemingly no hope. Working with this individual to get her paperwork filled out for assistance for the three months in question was by far easier than filling out the paperwork for the eviction process … and a lot less costly than the attorneys fees associated therein. Several months later she was able to secure another position. Although her new job was for less pay and required a little further travel, she went back to work, smiling a lot more and made every effort to get the rent in on time once again. As I write this chapter, it has been more than two years since this situation, and although I did have to wait a while, at this time I have not had a single month where this apartment has not produced an income for me.

Worst case situations—disappearing tenants, abandonment, refusal to pay rent, destroying property, can prove to be more difficult. Careful attention in the vetting process can help you avoid untold issues here. If you find yourself involved with any of these types of issues, legal action is the only course of action available. If you must enter an apartment you suspect has been abandoned, bring a police officer with you as a witness. Record everything you do, date, time, who, what, when and get all this to your attorney and wait for the legal proceeding to move forward. You will win a judgment for your losses, but you need to proceed within the confines of the law. These situations are not the time to be cocky or abrasive, they must be handled properly or you will bring the full extent of the law upon yourself. Have an attorney ready should you ever need him or her.

Now, I realize that last paragraph will scare some folks, especially the thought of dealing with the law or attorneys. But this is America and lawyers are everywhere. No investment is safe or free of the industry of law.

I have this section here for a reason.

A lot of what I have ever read on real estate investing is designed to teach you how to write a lease, how to get out of something that you manage to get yourself into, and even to "bake a loaf of bread in the oven before showing an apartment to prospective tenants" to give that homey scent.

Please.

In everything you will ever do there is a degree of risk and a measure of work. This section is here for you to take a close look at yourself to see if you should even bother reading further. If you don't have the proper demeanor, don't become a landlord. Save tenants the trouble and buy stock instead. If you can deal with and truly enjoy working with people, if you are not afraid to help them from time to time and actually enjoy the concept of win-win, then by all means, read on.

I do need to explain one other little thing first. In my humble opinion, one of the biggest problems facing most non-professional landlords, (those owning small two or three multi-family homes) is a lack of discipline. If you have $10,000 to invest in rental property, you must make sure you have enough cash on hand to weather any storms or delays in order to meet your obligations. You must have the discipline to understand that expenses will increase at exactly the same time that income decreases—always—not just sometimes. If any of the worst case scenarios come to fruition, you will have legal fees, court fees, repair and advertising fees, and more. These will likely happen at exactly the same time there is no income coming in from that apartment. Therefore, discipline yourself to bank most of the income you receive from tenants and build a Reserve Fund which we will talk about in the next section. This will ensure you are covered for any situation that comes along. It is an absolute necessity.

Even when things go well, like when a tenant leaves after ten years because they are finally able to buy a home of their own (the single best reason to lose a tenant), at the same moment you fail to get a rent check, you will be handing back a security deposit. It is absolutely amazing to me how many landlords believe the security deposits are gifts. Unprepared to return the funds, they look for any excuse to hold the deposit and an increasing number of tenants have to take a landlord to small claims court to get it back.

This tendency to run the properties as a cash machine instead of a business is a blueprint for failure. As such, it is a different breed of people who seem to invest in real estate than the stock market. Most of the people who invest in Wall Street are deposit and forget, compounding the interest and earnings for greater future growth potential. For the amateur real estate investor, (including many who attest to being professional) it seems to be more hand to mouth—the tenant's hand to landlord's mouth.

The amateur will usually find they have waited too long to make necessary repairs and simple repairs become emergency repairs for which they have no financial means to address. These things become costly in two distinctly separate but highly related ways. First, the cost of emergency repairs is always higher, and second, the quality of the repair made in haste will not survive as long as a carefully planned and well executed repair. There is a saying, "Never make a repair if you can make an improvement for the same cost." When time and planning are on your side, resulting improvements will enhance the value of the property. When need and haste envelope you, errors and omissions rob you of opportunity. Heating systems

> **The cost of emergency repairs is always higher than regular maintenance.**

do not break down in summer, but they frequently fail on holiday weekends with guests from Europe. Stressful times are prime-time for failures of the ill-prepared.

Take a hard look at yourself and make sure you are willing to make a commitment before continuing. Not buying real estate may be the best thing you could do if you don't have the right demeanor. By the same token, buying real estate can be the most lucrative thing you could do as well. Only you can identify on which side of the fence you belong.

If you decide you are indeed suited, then the rest of this book is dedicated to the proper way to accomplish just that.

If you don't
have the right
demeanor, not
buying real
estate may be
the best thing
you could do.

# Part III

## B U S I N E S S
## A C U M E N

No two properties are alike, property transactions are even more dissimilar. This section is devised to create a foundation for the understanding of things to look for while trying to ascertain the underlying value of a property. Tax laws change, codes change, banking requirements change, policy pertaining to the business of realty, insurance and law also change. The information contained within the following pages was deemed as accurate as possible at the time it was written, but the reader must keep current with these changes on a continuous basis to ensure complete and accurate interpretation of materials presented and researched.

No guarantees are made or implied as to the success or failure of any project based on the content provided herein. There are almost always surprises following a real estate closing transaction, and while this information is designed to mitigate those surprises, it is not a replacement for due diligence and detailed investigation. *Caveat Emptor.*

CHAPTER NINE

# Relationships

Where the car dealer is primarily interested in the commission from the sale of the car you buy, your real estate agent is first and foremost interested in the *potential* commission you represent from the purchase of the property you seek. They attend classes and seminars and collect three-letter designations visibly indicating their experience, not so much to impress you but to reduce the time span between the commission checks they receive. The more knowledgeable they become, the more situations they can work through, and the more commissions they can make. Why else would they be in business? Rarely will you find a car salesman or a real estate agent who is interested in nurturing you for the long term. In the back of their mind there is always the notion that you will relay the experience you had in dealing with them to others along the way, hoping that positive communication will foster additional leads, but the commission is the here and now and as such is the priority.

A car salesman is unlikely to give you a special deal to entice you to buy your next car from him five years later. If you should find such a person, they probably won't last all that long in the firm they are with simply because of the nature of the business. Each salesman competes against all the others in the dealership for total sales figures, just as real estate agents compete for volume sales dollars within the agency. In some cases, year-end bonuses are contingent upon these figures and the competition is fierce. You then are ultimately reduced to a tool to help meet that end. As soon as the agent gets the idea you are not a serious buyer they will not waste any time entertaining you. This is not at all unnatural and you have to understand what you represent to them; their bread and butter. They are in business not to consummate a life-long friendship with you, but to feed their families.

Observe the central theme to the things I've been discussing. Knowledge and understanding of the how and why people are in the businesses they are in gives you the added benefit of being able to adjust your attitude. You want something from people and in exchange they want something from you, in this case, a commission. Practice the win-win outlook in everything you do.

> **Practice the win-win outlook in everything you do.**

You will notice a major transformation as you climb the corporate structure of the firms you work with. Real estate brokers and car dealerships own their companies and as owners they are naturally more concerned about your experience with their firms. Nothing undermines potential business than being bad-mouthed by disgruntled customers. Repeat business and word of mouth, (your portrayal of their firm to others) can affect their bottom line. Your experience matters. It is a sort of check and balance system, the owners desire to net out good reviews, and this requires that they keep their agents and salespeople in check. Both real estate brokers and car dealerships will look out for you for the long term relationship, but the sales agents tend to come and go much more easily.

# WHO WORKS FOR WHOM?

With that in mind understand this, neither real estate agents nor car salesman work for you. This can be extremely confusing for first time home buyers to grasp. As stated, real estate agents and car salespeople both work on commission and one would think they are similar, but our choice for comparison is very different in one very special way. Consider the cars on the dealer's lot and the inventory of properties for sale in the real estate agent's office. The car dealer owns (in partnership with the bank) each of the cars in the inventory. The real estate agent's firm, the broker, does not (generally) own any of the property in its inventory. They merely have signed agreements to represent the property owner of each to secure buyers for those properties.

The car salesperson is selling you a product and representing their boss while attempting to get the best price for the dealership. The real estate agent is legally bound to the home owner that is trying to sell. So if you try to buy a blue Toyota Camry with a grey leather interior and a sun roof and the dealer doesn't have one, he will eagerly look up the inventory of all the neighboring dealerships and find you one. When he does, the two dealers swap inventories and you get your choice vehicle. They do this because neither of them wants you buying a Nissan. The salesperson and the dealer work very hard to reach the best compromise with you. The best compromise in your eyes includes a variety of factors including lowest price, longest lease, and lowest interest rate and for the dealer, the highest price, extended warrantees, undercarriage rust-proofing, and the like. You negotiate back and forth until a compromise is reached and at that point a deal is consummated. The salesman earns a commission from his dealer and the dealer takes over to ensure a long term association is formed through service and follow-up calls.

In real estate the buying process often takes months and the real estate agent will get to know you first and foremost. They need to do this because many buyers will dictate all their needs and desires in a house and in the end purchase something totally different. You will have this individual working very diligently for you to find the perfect answer to your dream. In many cases they will seem to know you better than you know yourself. They listen to the list you have prepared, "I need to have a pool, garage, and master suite on the first floor." Then you end up buying a three story walkup townhouse with a Jacuzzi across from the tennis courts. Realtors ask a lot of questions and they make note of the reactions to things they point out. They watch your faces, watch your body language towards different features, and listen to all the unspoken nuances and mannerisms towards each other that communicates the differences between you. They are paying such attention because in order to close the deal they need to be able to show you and emphasize things you really want, not necessarily those things you *thought* you wanted. A good realtor converts you to a friend, then finds their friend a house.

At the point an agreement (called a binder) is signed to purchase a property, the agent you have been working with for months instantly becomes the paid agent of the seller and is obligated by law to get the best price for that seller. This convoluted arrangement has been a problem for a very long time for brokers, agents, sellers, and buyers alike.

The latest attempt to assuage the problem is with a signed agreement between the buyer and the agent called an "Exclusive Buyers' Agent Agreement." This is a form which was developed to protect the real estate agent from abuse by unscrupulous buyers, not as protection for the buyer. Understanding the purpose of the document requires understanding commissions. Imagine yourself as a real estate agent with the following scenario: you deal with some clients for months, finally find them the property they want only to learn they signed a purchase agreement their best friend's wife who also happens to be a realtor so she could get the commission. Exclusive Buyers' Agent Agreements are recent instruments to protect against such loss of services.

It should not be necessary but it happens entirely too often. Here's a simple rule, if you deal with an agent on a particular property do not speak to another agent about that property. Put yourself in the agents' shoes and you can see the issues regarding your commission. Working with a prospective client only to lose the commission to another agent does not bode well for anyone. Until you sign an exclusive buyers' agreement you are free to contact every listing agent there is until you find the one you feel most comfortable with. There is absolutely no need for you to be loyal to any particular agent or broker until you are ready to make an offer on a property or until you sign the agreement.

Realtors work very hard for the commissions they make and all too frequently those commissions evaporate at the last minute due to unforeseen circumstances, sometimes right at the closing table. They will make every attempt to befriend you, to gain your trust. This is not to trick you, but simply the tools necessary to better serve you, their customer. Agents and buyers may be working together for some time and it's best to nurture this as a professional relationship. If you are buying a property it is essential that you open up, help them to help you.

Many agents do not have a vast experience with income property and I generally deal directly with either the listing agent for the building I am interested in or the broker with whom I have the most trust. Brokers have been in the business longest, but don't expect direct access to them on your first quest. They are extremely busy people and won't have the time an agent will to teach you the basics. On the flip side, many agents will not have the necessary understanding of the basic investment strategies necessary to find good, high grade, investment properties that will meet the criteria that follow. Inexperienced agents will use the same basic thought process for investment purchases as they might for your dream home and as you reject property after property they may grow frustrated. Understand how the realty business works.

# THE SEARCH IS ON

There are many ways to locate potential properties and I usually start with www.realtor.com. You can search realtor.com properties in the comfort of your home without wasting gas or time. If I find something that looks interesting I will follow that search up with reviews on both www.trulia.com and www.zillow.com—both major assets in comparing the properties in the neighborhood. These will tell you tax histories, ownership histories, amenities, etc. All the sites have valuable information and there will be ample material to digest.

Once you have narrowed the search down to a few properties that seem to work on your spreadsheets (next chapter) and otherwise "look" interesting it's time to call the realtor.

Searching in this regard makes the choice of what realtor to call much easier as the name of the brokerage house as well as the listing agent will usually be on the page you are looking at. You won't even have to call, you can simply click on the "I am interested in the property" link and they will call you.

My suggestion at this point to you is to not have a realtor you speak to through such an arrangement send you information on "other properties" they feel you may be interested in. If they do and you end up speaking with the listing agent for that property later, you can very easily have both agents showing up looking for a commission if you make it to the closing. Not likely, but possible. Before you are ever going to be ready to call an agent to discuss any particular property you have to analyze that property first for the feasibility of whether or not it makes sense as a potential investment. For that, we evaluate the numbers.

Before we begin the next section, it is imperative you muster the capability to leave emotion at the door. Buying income producing real property is not the same as finding your dream house. You have no business speaking to a realtor, driving by, and most certainly not looking at a property until you know it works as the investment vehicle you are attempting to create! This is business. Park your feelings at the door.

There is no place
for emotion in
investment decisions.
Leave your emotion
at the door.

CHAPTER TEN

# The Numbers Game

As the investor, start any investment with an analysis of its potential value toward reaching your goals. How much income will the property command? What are the fixed expenses—taxes, insurance, licenses, and permits? What are the variable expenses—maintenance, advertising, and legal costs? What are the terms available for the purchase— mortgage rate, down payment requirement, and number of years to repay the loan? How much of a Return On Investment (ROI) will the property generate? These are the questions this chapter is designed to allow you to answer.

I have provided spreadsheets to create an easy-to-use process when analyzing potential investment properties. There are steps that should be followed in preparing these spreadsheets. You can visit my website to download these Excel spreadsheets for your own use (www.pritchardconsultinginc.com). Mathematical formulas are embedded throughout the spreadsheets to generate the correct responses for properly entered data based on the realtor's information you are given. Adjustments to all information can easily be accomplished to generate "What if?" scenarios for the properties we will explore in detail.

The spreadsheet has three primary areas of concern: income, expenses, and financing. An actual two family rental property was used in our first example which was advertised the day this chapter was written. I selected the property at random.

## Property Details

*Two family house with commercial zoning has loads of potential right in the heart of the village. Many updates include newer roof, siding and fencing, Priced to sell and has great potential to be a good income producing property.*

## General Information

| Beds | Not Available | Baths | Not Available |
|------|---------------|-------|---------------|
| House Size | 1,410 Sq. Ft. | Lot Size | 5,663 Sq. Ft. |
| Price | $149,000 | Price/Sq. Ft. | $106 |
| Property Type | Multi-Family | Year Built | 1900 |
| Neighborhood | Not Available | Style | Ranch |
| Stories | Not Available | Garage | Not Available |

## Property Features

- ✆ *Status: Active*
- ✆ *Approximately 0.13 acre(s)*
- ✆ *2 Total Unit(s)*
- ✆ *Type: Duplex*

- Lot Features: Estimated Annual Taxes are $4,763.00
- Lot size is less than 1/2 Acre
- Unit 1 is renting for $1,006.00
- Unit 1 has 6 Room(s)
- Unit 1 has 1 Full Bath
- Unit 1 has 3 Full Bedroom(s)
- Unit 1 features: Oven/Range, Refrigerator, Carpet in Kitchen and Living Room
- Unit 2 is renting for $636.00
- Unit 2 has 3 Room(s)
- Unit 2 has 1 Full Bath
- Unit 2 has 1 Bedroom
- Unit 2 features: Oven Range/Refrigerator, Kitchen, Living Room
- Complex Features: Cable, Existing Screens, 2 A/C Unit(s), 2 Electric Meter(s), 2 Gas Meter(s), 4 Parking Space(s)
- Heating Features: Natural Gas, Hot Water, 2 Heat Zone(s)
- Exterior Construction: Vinyl Siding, Frame
- Interior Features: Unfinished Basement/Basement
- Exterior Features: Blacktop Driveway, Comon Driveway, Circuit Breaker, Municipal Sewer, Municipal Sewer, Municipal Water, Gas Available

## *Blank Spreadsheet*

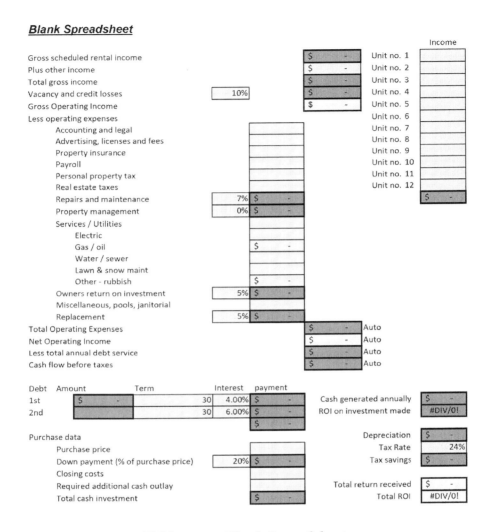

Table 10.1—Blank Spreadsheet

Once you have spotted a property that interests you, take the information from the listing and enter it onto the corresponding lines on the spreadsheet. Where the information is not present, you can do one of two things, 1) guess, or 2) search other databases like Trulia and Zillow. As you become more experienced, you will develop a "feel" for some of the things you need. Until then, create a process with clear steps you follow through with for every investment property you consider. Performing due diligence is a necessary step for every investment. In the end, you will likely "go with your gut," but verifying the listing information will help you make better decisions. For the sake of this exercise we will enter *only* the information asked for on the spreadsheet that is available on the listing we have selected.

### Property A - Spreadsheet 1

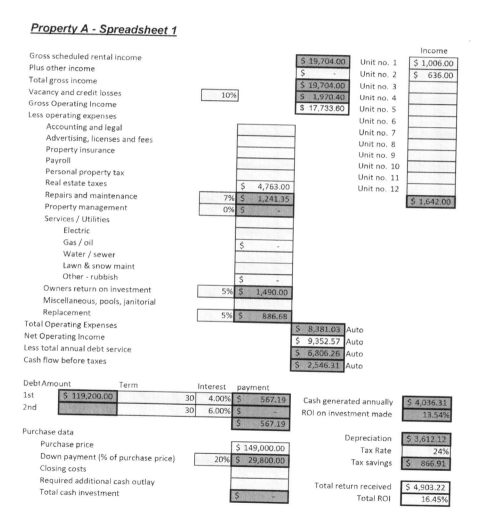

Table 10.2 Property A—Spreadsheet 1

In looking at the results we see this property suggests an overall return on investment of 16.45%. Not too bad, but there were several things missing—most notably as insurance, utilities, refuge and closing cost. Nothing on either www.trulia.com or www.zillow.com added information, but they did suggest confirmation of the taxes. As mentioned we can estimate for our purposes to see if the property might be worth looking any further and so we plug in a few guesses.

### Property A - Spreadsheet 2

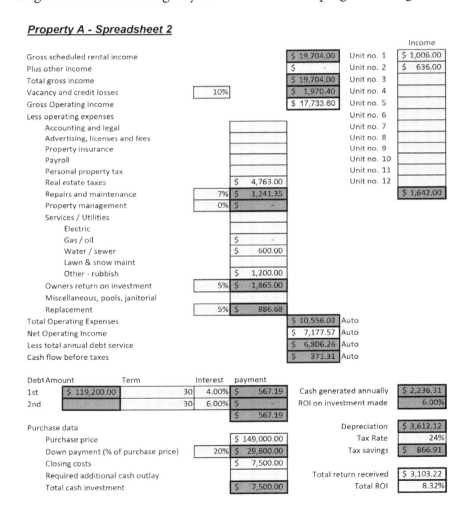

Table 10.3 Property A—Spreadsheet 2

Adding guesses is certainly not a scientific way of approaching whether we have a potentially valid property but it will help to weed out the trash from the possible gems. In this particular case a more careful reading of the listing we see the annotation that there are two electric meters and two gas meters. It is safe to assume the tenants are responsible for their own heat, cooking gas and electric so the bills should be minimal. We added $600.00 per year for the water and sewer but nothing for other utilities. We added $1,200 a year for the trash and assumed closing costs to be about 15% of the total and thus entered $7,500.00. The bottom line analysis reduces the overall ROI from 16.62% to 8.32% but there are other things to investigate and the numbers need not send us packing just yet and for two reasons.

First, the rent for the units is out of line. One unit is 6-room, 3-bedroom, the other is 3 rooms 1-bedroom. The rents should be a little closer than they are and a quick look through the local newspaper is all it takes to confirm what the rents in the area will command. In the paper this day for the village in question there are no 3 bedroom units advertised but there are two 1-bedroom units both asking $1,100.00 but both of these are advertising "heat and hot water included." We will talk more about this disparity later on but it is probably safe to assume $800.00 per month for the 1-bedroom unit. We will leave the other unchanged.

As it is unsafe to gamble, assume it will cost a few dollars to bring the unit to the required standard in order to receive that $800 per month and I have added $5,000 in the other costs column as an allowance. One last look at the upgraded spreadsheet will tell me whether or not I would ever call the realtor on this particular property.

## Property A - Spreadsheet 3

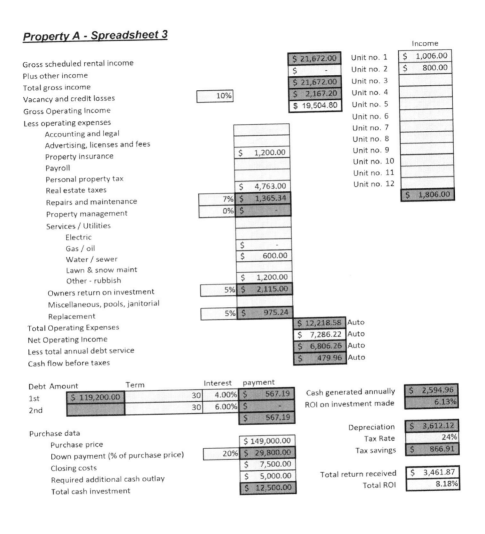

| | | | | Income | |
|---|---|---|---|---|---|
| Gross scheduled rental income | | $ 21,672.00 | Unit no. 1 | $ 1,006.00 | |
| Plus other income | | $ - | Unit no. 2 | $ 800.00 | |
| Total gross income | | $ 21,672.00 | Unit no. 3 | | |
| Vacancy and credit losses | 10% | $ 2,167.20 | Unit no. 4 | | |
| Gross Operating Income | | $ 19,504.80 | Unit no. 5 | | |
| Less operating expenses | | | Unit no. 6 | | |
|    Accounting and legal | | | Unit no. 7 | | |
|    Advertising, licenses and fees | | | Unit no. 8 | | |
|    Property insurance | | $ 1,200.00 | Unit no. 9 | | |
|    Payroll | | | Unit no. 10 | | |
|    Personal property tax | | | Unit no. 11 | | |
|    Real estate taxes | | $ 4,763.00 | Unit no. 12 | | |
|    Repairs and maintenance | 7% | $ 1,365.34 | | $ 1,806.00 | |
|    Property management | 0% | $ - | | | |
|    Services / Utilities | | | | | |
|       Electric | | | | | |
|       Gas / oil | | $ - | | | |
|       Water / sewer | | $ 600.00 | | | |
|       Lawn & snow maint | | | | | |
|       Other - rubbish | | $ 1,200.00 | | | |
|    Owners return on investment | 5% | $ 2,115.00 | | | |
|    Miscellaneous, pools, janitorial | | | | | |
|    Replacement | 5% | $ 975.24 | | | |
| Total Operating Expenses | | $ 12,218.58 | Auto | | |
| Net Operating Income | | $ 7,286.22 | Auto | | |
| Less total annual debt service | | $ 6,806.26 | Auto | | |
| Cash flow before taxes | | $ 479.96 | Auto | | |

| Debt Amount | Term | Interest | payment | | |
|---|---|---|---|---|---|
| 1st | $ 119,200.00 | 30 | 4.00% | $ 567.19 | Cash generated annually $ 2,594.96 |
| 2nd | | 30 | 6.00% | $ - | ROI on investment made 6.13% |
| | | | | $ 567.19 | |

| Purchase data | | |
|---|---|---|
| Purchase price | $ 149,000.00 | Depreciation $ 3,612.12 |
| Down payment (% of purchase price) | 20% $ 29,800.00 | Tax Rate 24% |
| Closing costs | $ 7,500.00 | Tax savings $ 866.91 |
| Required additional cash outlay | $ 5,000.00 | Total return received $ 3,461.87 |
| Total cash investment | $ 12,500.00 | Total ROI 8.18% |

### Table 10.4 Property A—Spreadsheet 3

With our overall ROI reduced to 8.18% this particular property still warrants further investigation. This was done by calling the listing agent found on the original Realtor.com page. We discussed confirmation of all the numbers previously entered on the spreadsheet. We also discussed the fact that this is a "short sale," meaning the property is being offered for less than the mortgage balance currently encumbering the property. The rents are what they are because the current owner "is a nice guy and doesn't want to raise the rent on nice tenants." That may or may not be the case, but the red flag for me was the amount being charged. Generally a private owner will not end up with rents such as $1,006.00 and $636.00 respectively. This would be more believable if the rents were rounded to $1,000.00 and $650.00. The indication is these are subsidized tenants taking either housing assistance or welfare where the rents are set not by the landlord but the agency on behalf of the tenant. When asked I was told, "I don't think so." Water and sewer were "estimated" by the agent to be "about $600.00 a year" and I was told the insurance would be "about $1,200.00."

Because the sale is a short sale I was told that to pursue this property further would require a home inspection and financial commitment after a positive outcome to an initial visit to ascertain the general condition which I declined.

There was one additional point that requires explanation. In the description of the property is mention of "commercial zoning." This property is currently being utilized as a residential two-family but occupies a commercial site. Banks today have a very difficult time supporting a mortgage if the zone does not match the current use. This is because the mortgages are typically bundled together and sold to investors through Freddy Mac or Fannie Mae and the Federal regulations governing those packages have changed considerably. You could apply for a commercial loan however; commercial loans are very different than residential

**If the zone does not match the current use, banks are unlikely to support a mortgage.**

loans and considerably more expensive. Commercial property is not within the realm of what we are working on here and therefore this property is rejected; see the suggested reading list in the appendix. But there are other reasons for rejection as well and we will look at these as there is much to be gained educationally.

The property taxes were confirmed as being accurate by the realtor, however, a search of the county records showed the taxes for the latest year were in fact $7,270.25. This is 53% error. A call to the village clerk identified the refuge is indeed collected with the taxes but does not show on the county records as such since counties do not have to make good on village bills other than unpaid taxes. Add another $1,442.00 in undisclosed costs.

Rents on subsidized units cannot be increased until the annual review unless you are dismissing the current tenants and to do that you must have a sound legal reason for their removal. It was not indicated one way or the other as to whether the tenants were being subsidized; the question was ignored completely.

I don't mind people ignoring my question, it will all come out eventually! In this case, a final review of the spreadsheet with the most accurate numbers available nets a -2.80% ROI. This is after removing the additional $5,000.00 for upgrades and eliminating the increase to the rent.

Let's take a look at one last table to evaluate this property before moving on.

## Property A - Spreadsheet 4

|  | | Income |
|---|---|---|
| Gross scheduled rental income | $ 19,704.00 | Unit no. 1 — $ 1,006.00 |
| Plus other income | $ - | Unit no. 2 — $ 636.00 |
| Total gross income | $ 19,704.00 | Unit no. 3 |
| Vacancy and credit losses — 10% | $ 1,970.40 | Unit no. 4 |
| Gross Operating Income | $ 17,733.60 | Unit no. 5 |
| Less operating expenses | | Unit no. 6 |
| Accounting and legal | | Unit no. 7 |
| Advertising, licenses and fees | | Unit no. 8 |
| Property insurance | $ 1,200.00 | Unit no. 9 |
| Payroll | | Unit no. 10 |
| Personal property tax | | Unit no. 11 |
| Real estate taxes | $ 7,270.25 | Unit no. 12 |
| Repairs and maintenance — 7% | $ 1,241.35 | |
| Property management — 0% | $ - | $ 1,642.00 |
| Services / Utilities | | |
| Electric | | |
| Gas / oil | $ - | |
| Water / sewer | $ 800.00 | |
| Lawn & snow maint | | |
| Other - rubbish | $ 1,442.00 | |
| Owners return on investment — 5% | $ 1,865.00 | |
| Miscellaneous, pools, janitorial | | |
| Replacement — 5% | $ 886.68 | |
| Total Operating Expenses | $ 14,705.28 | Auto |
| Net Operating Income | $ 3,028.32 | Auto |
| Less total annual debt service | $ 6,806.26 | Auto |
| Cash flow before taxes | $ (3,777.94) | Auto |

| Debt Amount | | Term | Interest | payment | | | |
|---|---|---|---|---|---|---|---|
| 1st | $ 119,200.00 | 30 | 4.00% | $ 567.19 | Cash generated annually | $ (1,912.94) |
| 2nd | | 30 | 6.00% | $ - | ROI on investment made | -5.13% |
| | | | | $ 567.19 | | |

| Purchase data | | | | |
|---|---|---|---|---|
| Purchase price | $ 149,000.00 | Depreciation | $ 3,612.12 |
| Down payment (% of purchase price) — 20% | $ 29,800.00 | Tax Rate | 24% |
| Closing costs | $ 7,500.00 | Tax savings | $ 866.91 |
| Required additional cash outlay | | Total return received | $ (1,046.03) |
| Total cash investment | $ 7,500.00 | Total ROI | -2.80% |

## Table 10.5 Property A—Spreadsheet 4

There are a considerably large number of things to gain from this exercise and the most important is the value of your time. This property, the five spreadsheets, the online verifications, and the call to the realtor took less than 40 minutes start to finish. Add another twenty minutes to browse realtor.com and we'll call it an hour. This is extremely important as you do not want this to become a full time job. Nor does it need to be. Understandably it will take you a little longer until you are comfortable with what to look for and look out for but if you practice evaluating properties you will be amazed at how quickly you understand it.

One a day will make you quite astute in a very short time. I used to brown bag it to work and look at potential properties during lunch. I found many worthy properties during a quiet lunch and set up appointments to look at several prospects on the way home. Being an hour late getting home seems worth it in retrospect when you start earning $8,000.00 a year in discretionary income for doing it.

CHAPTER ELEVEN

# Evaluating the Numbers

In the last chapter we ran a scenario on a test property. We made some guesses where we needed to, and plugged a bunch of seemingly random numbers in certain spots on our spreadsheet in order to spit out a result. Essentially, based on what numbers you put in where, you can influence the result to have it back up whatever feelings you have about the property. You have complete control. Numbers can be manipulated—ask anyone who has created a pie chart to demonstrate profit and loss.

What does evaluating the numbers mean? It means getting to the bottom line.

In chapter 6 we discussed vacancy factors well below 5%, yet in our spreadsheet we had a vacancy factor of 10%. The numbers indicated our maintenance costs at 7% and a replacement rate of 5% (which we never even discussed)! We also plugged in the asking price for the property without any suggestion of what our actual offer for the property might be.

The numbers tell the story. You are determining the value of the property—to you—which has little to do with the asking price. You are simply looking for the difference between what comes in and what goes out to determine whether or not what remains is worth your time, trouble, and investment capital. Each of these impacts the bottom line. There are essentially two sides to the story. As a business model it would be considered Revenue Stream and Cost Structure. Every dollar increase on the Revenue Stream (rent and other income) and every dollar of reduction on the Cost Structure (Operating Expenses) has a profound effect on the bottom line. This effect is in multiples of every dollar saved and every dollar received. You should have a greater understanding of why this is by the end of the chapter.

The bottom line is transformed into a value for the building and the terms for payment—the mortgage. Value is not what sellers are asking for the building, and it is not the amount you are willing to pay for the building because you like it. Value is based on the income less the expenses factored by the terms of the loan agreement. For this reason, the price the building is listed for is totally irrelevant. If the numbers worked into the spreadsheet allow a nice return on your investment, then negotiating a good price can only increase that margin for you. First you need to determine the most you would be willing to pay for the property in question. Then negotiate a better price (if possible), but once you agree the investment is indeed the viable choice, do not climb above your set price.

This section will be helpful to you as a reference when first looking at properties. We will look at items that need to go into the spreadsheet and then we will run a few scenarios with explanation as to how and why we did the things we did. Review the blank spreadsheet and play with it until you are comfortable.

## Blank Spreadsheet

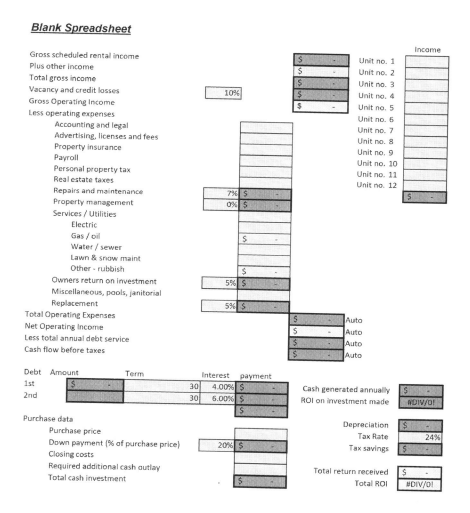

## Table 11.1 Blank spreadsheet

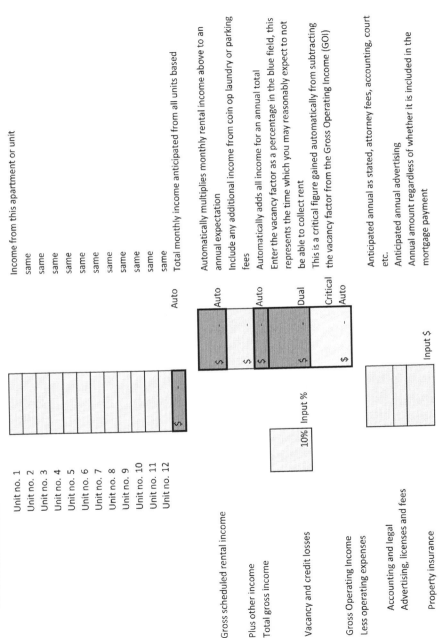

**Table 11.2—Blank Spreadsheet with Explanations**

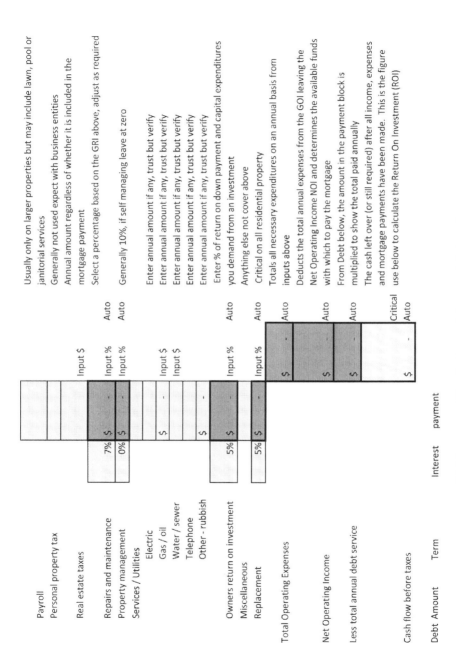

| Item | | | | | Explanation |
|---|---|---|---|---|---|
| Payroll | | | | | Usually only on larger properties but may include lawn, pool or janitorial services |
| Personal property tax | | | | Input $ | Generally not used expect with business entities |
| Real estate taxes | | | | | Annual amount regardless of whether it is included in the mortgage payment |
| Repairs and maintenance | 7% | $ | - | Input % | Select a percentage based on the GRI above, adjust as required |
| Property management | 0% | $ | - | Input % | Generally 10%, if self managing leave at zero |
| Services / Utilities | | | | | |
| Electric | | $ | - | Input $ | Enter annual amount if any, trust but verify |
| Gas / oil | | | | Input $ | Enter annual amount if any, trust but verify |
| Water / sewer | | | | | Enter annual amount if any, trust but verify |
| Telephone | | | | | Enter annual amount if any, trust but verify |
| Other - rubbish | | $ | - | | Enter annual amount if any, trust but verify |
| Owners return on investment | 5% | $ | - | Input % | Enter % of return on down payment and capital expenditures you demand from an investment |
| Miscellaneous | | | | | Anything else not cover above |
| Replacement | 5% | $ | - | Input % | Critical on all residential property |
| Total Operating Expenses | | $ | - | Auto | Totals all necessary expenditures on an annual basis from inputs above |
| Net Operating Income | | $ | - | Auto | Deducts the total annual expenses from the GOI leaving the Net Operating Income NOI and determines the available funds with which to pay the mortgage |
| Less total annual debt service | | $ | - | Auto | From Debt below, the amount in the payment block is multiplied to show the total paid annually |
| Cash flow before taxes | | $ | - | Critical / Auto | The cash left over (or still required) after all income, expenses and mortgage payments have been made. This is the figure use below to calculate the Return On Investment (ROI) |

| Debt | Amount | Term | Interest | payment |
|---|---|---|---|---|

**Table 11.2 — Blank Spreadsheet with Explanations**

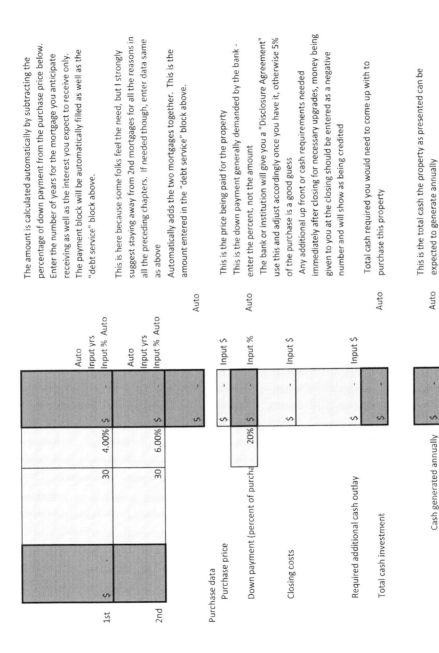

**Table 11.2—Blank Spreadsheet with Explanations**

The amount is calculated automatically by subtracting the percentage of down payment from the purchase price below. Enter the number of years for the mortgage you anticipate receiving as well as the interest you expect to receive only. The payment block will be automatically filled as well as the "debt service" block above.

This is here because some folks feel the need, but I strongly suggest staying away from 2nd mortgages for all the reasons in all the preceding chapters. If needed though, enter data same as above

Automatically adds the two mortgages together. This is the amount entered in the "debt service" block above.

This is the price being paid for the property

This is the down payment generally demanded by the bank - enter the percent, not the amount

The bank or institution will give you a "Disclosure Agreement" use this and adjust accordingly once you have it, otherwise 5% of the purchase is a good guess

Any additional up front or cash requirements needed immediately after closing for necessary upgrades, money being given to you at the closing should be entered as a negative number and will show as being credited

Total cash required you would need to come up with to purchase this property

This is the total cash the property as presented can be expected to generate annually

| | | |
|---|---|---|
| Represented ROI on investment made | #DIV/0! | Auto | This is the return on the investment made on an annual basis and is the percentage of annual income expected from the total cash investment made purchasing the property including down payment, closing costs and any additional cash outlays |
| Depreciation | $ - | Auto | The amount of annual tax depreciation expected from the property |
| Tax Rate | $ 0.24 | | Your current tax rate |
| Tax savings | $ - | Auto | The anticipated savings from your other, regularly earned income, that owning this property will save you annually. |
| Total return received | $ - | Auto | The total return including the tax savings |
| Total ROI | #DIV/0! | Critical | The total ROI on the overall investment, this is the figure you examine to determine the feasibility of the overall project. |
| | | Auto | |

Table 11.2—Blank Spreadsheet with Explanations

Populating the spreadsheet is the first objective. In the end it will be completed factually. All estimates should be replaced with verifiable figures. It often takes many times to complete accurately and sometimes the numbers themselves are not the only reason for acceptance or rejection. We will start at the top of the spreadsheet and work our way down line by line. Many of the lines will be left blank as they do not apply to all properties.

# UNIT INCOME

Income has a separate column for each rental unit. In the individual unit lines enter the current stated monthly income for each apartment or other rental space. In some cases you may find a building that has a two bay garage that is (or can be) rented separately. Just because the current landlord does not rent garage spaces separately does not mean you cannot, especially if there is already ample parking for the tenants. If the current landlord is overlooking a potential source of income, which happens more than you may think, don't advertise your intentions. Work the spreadsheet with their numbers as a tool to negotiate a good deal. Use their numbers to negotiate a good price. Utilize and initiate your real spreadsheet after you close the deal. People can get paid very handsomely for their ideas, the same goes for woefully low rents. Build your spreadsheet to understand the value to you *after* you make necessary changes. It is not lying and it is not cheating, it is simply being smarter than they are. They could have done these things but either chose not to, or never thought of it.

Monthly rent in the eyes of the landlord is the income the unit is expected to generate. The look through the eyes of the tenant is not the same. The tenants will calculate their living expenses as a whole. What they can afford to pay as rent is based upon other variables for such things as heat, electric, garbage, parking etc. When comparing advertisements of similar units to get a good idea on the market, be sure to make note of things like "heat and hot water included." If your apartments have separate meters, your tenants will pay for their own utilities, and your rent for the unit must account for this factor. Make sure you compare apples to apples.

## GROSS SCHEDULED RENTAL INCOME

Gross Scheduled Income is a combination of all the income the building generates from the unit rental income column. This is multiplied by twelve months to show the annual scheduled income and everything from here on will be represented in annual terms.

## PLUS OTHER INCOME

Rent is not the only source of income a property can generate. Coin-op laundry machines, paid parking, pet fees and interest … these all represent income from the building.

When I talk with a realtor or seller about a property, I ask what the income is per apartment and generally don't bother asking if there is any additional income. I've never met one who forgot to mention other income sources, and I will not plant the idea in their mind if they don't mention it. I'll find other potential sources for income when I walk the building and use any additional income I find as a cushion. However, if other income is represented on the listing or by the owner or agent, you will want full disclosure.

Demand records, receipts and statements for that income. Keep in mind that added income generally comes attached to higher maintenance costs. I rarely have anything in this category, but having coin-op laundry service in a building is a perk for tenants if washers and dryers are not in the apartments. It eliminates the need to haul their clothing to the local Laundromat each week. Perks make happy tenants and happy tenants rent from you longer.

Any income earned along this line has to be calculated annually not monthly. If the agent tells you the income from an on-site coin-op laundry is $50.00 per month, put in $600.00 for the 12 months.

# TOTAL GROSS INCOME

This is the total amount of all income sources identified for an entire year. Some realtors will advertise properties as 10 times gross income. For example, a building with $45,000 a year in gross income should sell for $450,000. Sounds easy. But that same building could range in expenses from as low as $12,000 a year to as high as $35,000 a year. It does not take a rocket scientist to understand what the difference means to your profitability. Ignore anyone trying to sell you property based on multiples of gross income.

# VACANCY AND CREDIT LOSSES

We then take into consideration a "Vacancy Factor" which varies greatly from state to state and community to community. My area has typically seen a vacancy factor of about 5% since I began in this business, but it has bounced between 4% and 7% depending on economic market conditions. I have had several years with no vacancies what-so-ever! This takes years to perfect. Don't expect it starting out. The spreadsheet is populated with 10% for this entry, and when an adjustment is needed, remember that it is the percentage that should be changed not the dollar amount. I find using 10% as a vacancy factor works well for planning purposes, especially on properties newly added to a portfolio as tenants need time to vet out landlords and are not always comfortable with change.

In the case where rents have been unnaturally low, you will lose some tenants when raising rents to more locally averaged levels. You want to be able to adjust this number downward over time and never want to have it increase. Increasing it means you expect to receive less of the projected rents, so work hard to decrease this percentage to as low a figure as possible but not during your initial projection stage. If you are scheduled to receive $40,000 per year in rental income and 5% is your projected vacancy factor then your income is ($40,000 - 5% = $38,000). If you are wrong and you have to increase your vacancy factor to 10%, then you have much less to work with to pay your bills and mortgage ($40,000 - 10% = $36,000). Avoid this by starting with a higher percentage.

There are effectively three necessary goals to be determined on this spreadsheet.

1. **Gross Operating Income (GOI)**

2. **Total Operating Expenses**

3. **Return on Investment (ROI)**

# 1. Gross Operating Income

Gross Operating Income is effectively the first of the three necessary goals of the spreadsheet. The sum of all the projected rental income plus any additional income there may be, as we stated above, equals Total Gross Income. Gross Operating Income therefore is the Total Gross Income less the vacancy factor and represents the amount you will have available to pay all the expenses and make your mortgage payments. This amount will be determined upon completion of the steps above.

# 2. Total Operating Expenses

Expenses are the compilation of all bills associated with the annual operation and upkeep of the property. Each line item should be carefully researched and entered as close to reality as possible. This is critical. In the example from the last chapter, if we were to add $1,000 to any expense line item, we would reduce the value of the property accordingly. Being accurate and honest about your expenses is vital to making a sound assessment of a property's profitability.

Some items on our sample spreadsheet may not apply to your specific situation, for instance legal and accounting. Unless you are purchasing as a partnership, or you plan on having evictions there should be no need for either legal or accounting expenses. Your personal income taxes at the end of the year simply need a schedule E attached, and if you pay someone to do your taxes it will cost you a little more to have this completed.

## ADVERTISING

This entry is a little tricky. In many cases the seller will list no advertising expense. That may very well be the case. I have two properties on main roads and 20 years ago purchased a few custom made metal signs with vinyl lettering advertising "Apartment for Rent" and my phone number. For these two properties I have never needed anything other than this advertising medium. In fact, for several years I have had no advertising fees at all. I have other properties not located on main streets that must be advertised to fill a vacancy. These properties require an annual advertising estimate. Where I need to advertise, I place ads in the local newspaper. I have found for me it is the only venue that works consistently, and I can pay for the ads for an entire month at a cost of about $280. I budget this amount for any one or two family property, assuming a 5% vacancy factor. Since we are using a 10% vacancy factor, our two family property could be expected to have one apartment vacant for 2.4 months. You will not be able to accurately assess the need for advertising until you visit the property. If it is not possible to sufficiently advertise from a window in the vacant apartment, then get a quote from the local paper for running an ad and use this amount for this line item. Double this amount for 3 or 4 family buildings. Putting a figure in for this line can always be removed later, but do not expect a seller to tell you he pays for advertising—even if he does.

# PROPERTY INSURANCE

To get a quote from your own insurance agent, you will need a little information from the realtor. They will be able to give you the section, lot, and block of the property along with the address, square footage, type and age of construction. This is all you should need to call and request a quote and an insurance agent can usually have one prepared for you in a few hours. Your quote will never be the same as the seller's (if they have anything listed at all). Just for the heck of it I called my agent for a quote on the sample property in the last chapter where we used $1,200 as the amount for property insurance, suggested by the real estate agent. The price from my insurance agent was $867.00.

There are fundamental differences regarding insurance for each property you consider. You need to evaluate the type and amount of insurance you need. As a matter of habit I have always used "full replacement value" and "loss of rents" is also critical. I recommend sitting down with an independent insurance agent as they are often able to get better deals for you than you could get for yourself. They know their business and they will shop your needs around to competing companies.

# PAYROLL

I have never needed a payroll line item; it is for larger properties where you might have an on-site property manager. This should remain blank for the foreseeable future until you have a respectable portfolio of properties. Once this happens, one employee can be brought on to handle multiple properties.

# PERSONAL PROPERTY TAX

This will generally fall in the same category as payroll. Until you grow in volume and open a management company, it should also be left blank. All your deductions can go against your schedule E until that time, and you should not have any taxes due when first starting out.

# REAL ESTATE TAXES

Depending on where you live, this is arguably the single largest line item entry you will have under expenses. The Office of the Assessor will get you the most current information, or once you learn to access them, county records are by far the easiest route. The quote given in the example in the last chapter took about five minutes to obtain on-line. There is no need to leave your house or office to obtain an accurate amount for real estate taxes.

There are usually multiple taxes that need to be added together, school, county and town, village and in some cases fire districts and libraries. The county is the source to have them all and one-stop-shopping is always easier.

# REPAIR AND MAINTENANCE

Repairs and maintenance on property depend on a few factors including the age of the building, the make-up of the tenancies (families with many young children vs. aging empty nesters), and your ability and availability to make minor repairs yourself.

The differences in the answers to these questions can be huge and deserve a close look. By far the most critical of these is your ability and availability to handle minor repairs. If you have to pay a handyman to tighten a door knob and hire a plumber to fix a dripping faucet, you will have a much higher figure in this line than another person who can do it themselves. Consider your answers and make sure there is an accurate reflection of reality in this line item. I was told when I first got into this business that this figure was based only on age and condition but experience has shown these to be of little relevance compared to your own involvement. Age has nothing to do with condition. Many European buildings have stood for hundreds of years, in some cases a thousand years, and with the proper care and feeding so will yours. How much you need to spend to keep up on these items is what we need to figure out here.

First we have to know what "repairs and maintenance" means. Repairs should include such things as replacing leaky faucets, broken door knobs, damaged sheetrock, broken cabinet doors, and repainting and cleaning vacant apartments. Maintenance should include such items as lawn maintenance, snow removal, sweeping the hallways, and replacing broken light bulbs. In addition, you must also account for preventative maintenance—making sure the foundation is water tight before leaks begin to develop, and fixing loose down spouts before they lead to wet basements.

Replacing old refrigerators, heating systems, roofs and carpet should not be included under repairs and maintenance; these are "replacement items" and have their own category which we will discuss shortly.

If you pick the rent up in person (as I like to do), sweeping the hallway while you are there takes but a couple of minutes. Checking for burned out bulbs takes the same amount of time. Asking the tenants how everything is will give you insight as to what has to be addressed, and if you are on it every month it won't add up. I mow my own lawns and have a snow blower for the driveways and walks. I no longer do any of my own plumbing, heating, or electrical work for two reasons: 1) I can afford to have people do it now, and 2) I was never very good at these things in the first place. I still do my own painting and sheetrock repairs whenever I have time.

If you do none of these things I would go as high as 15% for repairs and maintenance and if you are very handy 5% will cover you as long as you take care of the problems as they arise and don't procrastinate. The 7% we used in this example is a relatively happy median. Adjust the percentage as you feel necessary, but only after taking a good hard look at yourself.

The nature of the type of construction will also impact this entry. I recently stumbled across a three family property which had wooden fire escapes on three sides and four wooden decks. With the amount of wood exposed to the harsh weather conditions, a 50% maintenance factor may not have been enough. You have to be able to accurately assess the variables.

# P R O P E R T Y
# M A N A G E M E N T

Property management, if used, is generally 10% of the income received each month and is paid out monthly. Use the percentage against the Gross Operating Income for estimating purposes. The amount that is actually paid is based upon income received and not on Total Gross Income. If there is an empty apartment, no management fee is collected since no rent is received. This is a built in incentive program for the manager to get the place rented quickly. Be very careful to make sure the management company is properly vetting prospective tenants as the same incentives apply, the quicker it is rented, the higher the manager's income. Make sure the manager knows the lower the vacancy rate, the higher his income is and do not allow a bonus for getting the place filled.

I would also increase the repairs and maintenance line from 7% to 10% if you are using property management companies. They will not necessarily shop for the best price for you and often will add mark-ups to the repairs and maintenance being done on your behalf by their in-house contractors.

Doing things for yourself can be lucrative. In the book *Master Builders*, Paul Reichmann began an empire on the difference between what he spent building a warehouse and the lowest bid price contractors told him they would build it for. His total cost was $70,000 where the lowest bid came in at $125,000. People are in business to make money. So are you. The question thus becomes, do you want to make this money for you or for others?

If you are not capable of doing these things, then by all means a management company is viable as the alternative is to not own real estate. Handled properly it will still get you financial freedom; it may just take a little longer.

I am reaching the point in my life where serious consideration is being given towards management, but my plan is to start a management company as my own business and is a somewhat natural evolution.

So, if you are not hiring a management company, place zero on this line as the percentage.

If you are using a management company, place 10% in the management line entry and add three percentage points to the repairs and maintenance line entry. If you end up using a management company, make sure you read the contract very carefully and maintain vigilant oversight of all statements and work requests being done.

# SERVICES/UTILITIES

## Electric

In the example from the last chapter there were two units and only two electric meters. Each unit had its own entry and there were no "common areas" to both units. Common areas are defined as those areas such as a hallway or basement shared by multiple tenants, including those areas which tenants have no access. For common areas you will need to have an additional electric meter. Electric used in a common area cannot be part of the bill paid by any particular tenant without disclosure and a written agreement. This agreement should be entered into with the lease and must be very clear. Failure to inform a tenant that a portion of a bill they are required to pay is for areas not exclusively for their own use can cost you lost rent, legal fees, and a hefty bill to correct later. Knowing any issues and disclosing them are all it takes to eliminate a lot of headaches.

In the case of the example we used, the line item entry will be zero. There is no obligation for the landlord in this case, but is not the most common situation. You want to be concerned with the amount of all of the electric bills that the tenants pay as well as the ones you are responsible for. This is especially critical where the tenants pay their own electric heat, remember the tenants will calculate the housing costs they are willing or capable of paying per month inclusive of all housing related expenses. Rent is just a piece of the total.

Determine the amount you, as landlord, will be responsible for and enter this amount on the line (remember to calculate it as an annual figure).

## Gas/Oil

I like natural gas. There are few problems, it is easily separated to each unit, and there are no delivery issues like propane or oil. However, if you are in an area that does not have natural gas, your alternatives are limited. If natural gas is not available, the next best choice (from a landlord's perspective) is electric heat. Oil and propane are not as desirable as tenants may have to pay large sums up front to reimburse previous tenants for the remaining oil in the tanks, and these things are all considered hassles for tenants already steeped in the trouble of moving. Making it harder and more costly is not a good idea.

From the tenants' perspective, the best scenario is to have the landlord pay the heat (and the average is included in their rent). But that has other ramifications, and you must make the best business decision for you. Tenants know what they can afford, but there is another point to consider. Tenants are only going to be frugal with the lights and thermostat when they are paying the bills. A quick drive through town recording the open windows on a cold winter's day is all that is needed to see which apartment buildings have the landlords paying the heat.

My preference is to offer lower rent and have tenants be responsible to pay for their own heat and electric … every time … without hesitation.

If the tenants pay the heat great, leave the line at zero and make sure the rent accurately reflects the added burden to the tenant. Ask the agent for these figures in the early stages of the review process. Later on, if you find yourself getting more seriously involved in a prospect, demand twelve consecutive months of bills for every meter. Make sure the bills submitted for review are indeed consecutive, and all dated the same year.

If you as the landlord are expected to pay for the heat, you will need an accurate assessment up front. Ask for verification as early as possible. A call to the oil company will ensure there wasn't a mid-winter bill omitted from the figures. I will certainly make this call if I am only given two bills for the year, one in April and one in September. Common sense should tell you we don't use as much oil in the spring and summer months as is needed in the fall and winter months. Trust but verify, use whatever means are necessary.

Once you have ascertained the correct annual figures, enter this on the line for oil /gas. A zero is always best here.

## Water and Sewer

This is another intricate line item. I operate in a mostly rural area of the Hudson valley in New York. I have come across everything from well and septic tanks, to a well with municipal sewer connection, to having both municipal water and sewer available. Septic tanks have to be cleaned out regularly, and the costs need to be annotated. Well water is essentially free, and the electric for running the pump is included in the electric bill. Municipal water and sewer costs are calculated on the water side from reading the water meter and the sewer portion of the fee is based on that same meter, but as a separate line item entry. There is only a single bill. I have had a situation where a property was bought that had both water and sewer available in the street, but also had a well. The building's previous owner had connected to the sewer line, but had never connected to the water main, continuing to use the well. This was the best possible scenario as the there was no water meter from which to charge for the sewer connection. The total bill was exactly $10.00 per month for a four family property. That was the entry on the water/sewer line we used for over 21 years, $120.00. It never changed.

That happened just once—I never expect to see this situation again, and it is included here only to show you the variables you can encounter.

Municipal water and sewer is the best value for the money. It is carefree and can be easily budgeted for, but like heat, tenants who do not have a water bill to pay will not be self-conscience of how much they use. They may not tell you about leaks until it affects their water pressure, and they will wash the car and fill a child's pool each week.

I have taken to remedying this problem by putting in separate meters wherever possible and practicable. The bills come to me and I present them to the tenants for reimbursement each quarter as they come in. It is expensive to do initially, but I find it interesting that water bills that average $400.00 each quarter for a 4-family house drops to an average of only $247.00 a quarter when they are given the bills. I calculate the individual return on an investment made in doing this separation based on the total cost to install over the annual savings of the bills paid prior to doing the separation. In the last building where I separated water meters, I saved roughly $1,600 a year by paying a plumber $3,826.00 for the job, (there were already 4 separate hot water heaters in the building). The direct return on this investment was 42% ($1,600 / $3,826). I will have 100% of that money returned in just over two years.

There is one additional thing that needs to be considered with all of the line items under "expenses," and that is the relationship reducing expenses has to the value of the property as an investment vehicle. Think back to chapter 3 and our discussion of investment options. The difference between interest rates paid by junk bonds and government EE bonds is huge, but so to was the difference in risk. In order to have a high return I needed to buy a high risk bond and I have to balance my desired return against my risk comfort level. What If I could buy a bond where the opposite were true? What if I could buy lowest possible risk by securing only the highest possible return? This is essentially what we are doing here. Every dollar saved on an expense allows a higher mortgage to be paid from the Gross Operating Income GOI once the bills are paid.

Every dollar increase in Total Gross Income does the same as every dollar in reduced expense. Every dollar reduction in vacancy factor as well. In short, each dollar you either increase income or reduce expenses by will amortize $17.46 in mortgage value (based on 4% over 30 years). This means a mortgage borrowing a grand total of just $17.46 will cost $0.08 per month in a mortgage payment at 4% annual interest over 30 years. Multiplied this monthly payment of $0.08 by 12

**The greater the income stream generated, the higher the value of the investment.**

months will result in a total mortgage payment of exactly $1.00 per year. Thus a savings of $1,600 per year will allow payments to be made on a mortgage $27,936 more than could be otherwise supported. Mathematically it looks as such: $27,936 @ 4% interest for 30 years = $133.37 per month and, $133.37 per month x 12 months = $1,600 per year, give or take a coupe of pennies. Since investments are all essentially the purchase of an income stream the greater the income stream generated, the higher the value of the investment. As you will see in the next chapter this effect is directly translated to the value of the building and your overall investment return.

For the purposes of this chapter though we assume that any errors you make in not correctly annotating an expense will cause you to overpay for the property by the same amounts as the gains identified here and that is what we do not want to happen.

It may very well not be practical to separate the water without causing a lot of repairs to walls and such, but consider it as an option.

Use the annual amounts given to you by the agent for entry into this line. Where it is all municipal, the office of the clerk should have actual figures to compare to. Should the prospect of separating water meters come to mind don't mention to anyone at this time as the prospect will tighten up negotiation possibilities later on.

## Lawn and Snow

Lawn care and snow removal are items you cannot afford to overlook. Do them yourself or have them done as cheaply as possible. I do these chores myself and thus leave the entry blank. It may be that from time-to-time I hire people for these tasks, but it is not the norm. It is important to understand that all but one of the buildings I currently own are within walking distance of my residence, so I don't travel any distance to take care of them. Enter whatever figures you need, quotes are readily available from neighborhood maintenance folks.

## Other/Rubbish

I find people talk trash when it comes to refuse bills. This is almost always the case except if included in the taxes by municipalities. Even then it is too easy to simply say "it is in the taxes," but it is not always documented so that it will show up on the tax bill. You must verify this expense. It is not a variable like lawn maintenance, you cannot do this yourself, and therefore it will affect your bottom line. Get it right.

In municipalities where the property owner is responsible, you can get several quotes and pick the best price. These require you to pay monthly and continuously shop for the best price as competition will cause constant undercutting to get your business, then raise the fees annually knowing many people, once they have a service, stay the course. Either way, I like it included with the taxes, nothing to do but make sure the tenants' get the trash into the cans. But you must get the correct amount in the line item.

I have yet to use the "Other" part of the line, but you never know. It's there if you need it.

This concludes the Services/Utilities portion of the Expenses. These are probably the most important variables to consider and require the most attention. We will discuss more about why this is in the chapter, "Manipulating the Numbers."

# RETURN ON INVESTMENT

There should be no reason to buy an investment—any investment—without expecting to get a return on that investment. Cash in the bank, bonds, stock, bullion, or real estate. This particular line entry is an automated entry based on the interest rate you desire from the investment you are making. I have 5% in the block, but you can change it as you desire.

The investment you are making is the sum total of down payment, closing costs, and capital improvements. Total these together and multiply by the desired rate of return. This rate should be synonymous with the return you would demand of any investment where you would put the same amount of hard-earned cash.

The "pay yourself first" principal applies here. You are not buying a home to live in, you are making real estate investment with a set purpose. Earning money is the purpose.

# MISCELLANEOUS

This might include things like pool maintenance or other such amenities. Though you will need to make sure the insurance quotes reflect the added liability. I have yet to need this line entry.

# REPLACEMENT

Replacement schedules are probably the one thing that most landlords ignore and they are the one thing I feel are most important to the successful management of rental income property for the long term.

Repairs and maintenance are necessary entries, but eventually things get beyond repair and need to be replaced or upgraded. Replacing a worn out heater, weathered roof, or threadbare carpet is something you should budget for from the beginning. These should be prepared for based on the life expectancy of the unit.

See the replacement table which follows.

| Reserve for Replacement | | | | | | | | | |
|---|---|---|---|---|---|---|---|---|---|
| Loc | Cost | Item | Years | per month | Replaced in | Replace in | R2 In | Req. O.H. | |
| 1 $ | 400.00 | Stove | 7 | $ 4.76 | Jan-06 | Dec-12 | -1 | $ 404.44 | $ 400.00 |
| 2 $ | 400.00 | Stove | 7 | $ 4.76 | Jan-96 | Dec-02 | -123 | $ 984.29 | $ 400.00 |
| 3 $ | 400.00 | Stove | 7 | $ 4.76 | Jan-97 | Dec-03 | -111 | $ 926.19 | $ 400.00 |
| 1 $ | 500.00 | Refrigerator | 7 | $ 5.95 | Oct-11 | Sep-18 | 69 | $ 89.09 | $ 89.09 |
| 2 $ | 500.00 | Refrigerator | 7 | $ 5.95 | Jan-96 | Dec-02 | -123 | $ 1,230.36 | $ 500.00 |
| 3 $ | 500.00 | Refrigerator | 7 | $ 5.95 | Mar-12 | Mar-19 | 74 | $ 56.75 | $ 56.75 |
| 2 $ | 500.00 | Dish washer | 7 | $ 5.95 | Jan-98 | Dec-04 | -98 | $ 1,085.32 | $ 500.00 |
| E $ | 700.00 | Hot Water Heater | 7 | $ 8.33 | Jan-05 | Dec-11 | -13 | $ 809.17 | $ 700.00 |
| 1 $ | 5,000.00 | Furnace / ac | 20 | $ 20.83 | Jan-05 | Dec-24 | 145 | $ 1,977.78 | $ 1,977.78 |
| 2 $ | 5,000.00 | Furnace / ac | 20 | $ 20.83 | Jan-05 | Dec-24 | 145 | $ 1,977.78 | $ 1,977.78 |
| 3 $ | 5,000.00 | Furnace / ac | 20 | $ 20.83 | Jan-05 | Dec-24 | 145 | $ 1,977.78 | $ 1,977.78 |
| E $ | 10,000.00 | Roof | 25 | $ 33.33 | Jan-01 | Dec-25 | 157 | $ 4,760.00 | $ 4,760.00 |
| 3 $ | 1,000.00 | Carpet | 7 | $ 11.90 | Jan-01 | Dec-07 | -62 | $ 1,735.71 | $ 1,000.00 |
| | | | | $ 154.17 | | | | $ 18,014.64 | $ 14,739.17 |

## 11.3 Sample Replacement Table

The items that should be included in this list are furnaces and air conditioning units, hot water heaters, refrigerators, stove, microwaves, dishwashers, carpets, and roofs. The cost of these should be estimated along with a suggested life expectancy in years. As you get further along in your approach towards closing on a property, it will be important to evaluate the quality, condition, and age of the assets on your replacement table. If you purchase a building and have an inspection done where the roof is going to need to be replaced in 5 years, you had better make sure you have the funds on hand at that time to cover this cost. You do this by estimating the cost and verifying the age for each of these items at the time you close on the building and set aside a lump sum amount of money from your rental income to cover these expenses. From there it is simple math and a spreadsheet will calculate the amount needed on a monthly basis.

The example shown in the Replacement Table is a building currently in my possession for 30 years and it has a lot of **bold type**. The **bold** in this case is not a bad thing. It simply means that the unit has now exceeded the life expectancy or original design life from abuse that some tenants can apply to your property.

There are two significant things to keep in mind while studying this chart. First, if I hit only the minimum life expectancies of every item on the list, I need to deposit just $155.56/month into a money market or similar saving account to ensure I meet these requirements. The second pertains to all those items in bold. If you look at the line that states Loc 2 Refrigerator, you will notice it was replaced in Jan. 96. That is 18 years of service I have received from a unit that was given a 7 year life expectancy. It is estimated to cost $500.00 new. A seven year life is 84 months. A cost of $500.00 spread over 84 months is $5.95 per month and that deposit has been made for those 84 months as well as an extra 123 months. There is as of today $1,230.36 available for the purchase of a $500.00 unit. I can replace this unit at any time and reset the clock and the balance required on hand to zero. I could go out tomorrow and replace it, but why would I as long as it is still operating fine? I will, however, as it continues to age gracefully, check on it every few months to make sure it is indeed still running.

Any time something moves beyond the life expectancy I highlight it and perform these regular inspections to ensure it is running smoothly. I look for telltale signs of pending failure, but do not replace them until they begin to show such signs. I try to replace an operating unit prior to failure especially when good sales are being run. Roofs overdue are inspected annually and tenants are asked to immediately let me know of any water stains.

When you are first buying a new building you need to evaluate the age of all the above and ascertain the condition. You need to make an educated guess as to the number of years left before replacement becomes necessary. You can easily backdate the items on the list to the approximate date of installation and let the math work the table out from there. The bottom line is you should establish seed money for the replacement table at the time you purchase the property. Set the money aside and don't touch it for anything other than its projected need according to your table.

**Establish seed money for replacement at the time you purchase property.**

This means that if you were in the market for that 2 family property in the previous chapter, you would need not only the down payment plus the closing costs, but you should also have on hand the projected replacement cost as determined by the age of the equipment on your list at the time of closing. In the case of the 3 family in the spreadsheet shown, you would not need to have any funds in excess of the cost of the actual items, in other words there would be no reason to have $1,280.36 to cover the cost of a $500.00 refrigerator but you should have, in this case, half of $14,739.17 readily available to either seed future replacements or to be able to replace each item exceeding current life expectancies.

As far as the line item entry is concerned, I use 5% and it's fairly accurate. Later on when you get close to closing, you will replace this percentage with an actual figure calculated from the table you will establish.

Every building you purchase should cover the cost of every item being repaired, maintained, and replaced at any given time for that building. You will sleep better knowing this money is available and you will be able to better serve your tenants. This is the enticement for them to continue to stay in your building. There is an important and quite lucrative purpose behind establishing replacement accounts which we will delve further into in chapter 14. This spreadsheet is available for download on my web site www.pritchardconsultinginc.com.

# TOTAL OPERATING EXPENSES

Each of the line item entries under the category of expenses is added together to give you the Total Operating Expenses for the building you are considering for purchase. The line is not adjustable. It is a non-variable amount arrived at by adding all of the relevant entries and giving you the annual outlay the building will incur.

This marks the end of the Total Operating Expenses and begins parameters for determining return on investment

# NET OPERATING INCOME (NOI) or NET ICOME BEFORE DEBT SERVICE (NIBDS)

Net Operating Income (NOI) is the figure you have been working towards determining, and is generated by subtracting the Total Operating Expenses from the Gross Operating Income established earlier.

Gross Operating Income and Total Operating Expenses are required to determine the final category Return on Investment which which we will look at now.

# 3. Return on Investment

## LESS TOTAL ANNUAL DEBT SERVICE

The next area of discussion is the percentage of the building purchase price that will consist of other people's money, or the amount to be financed by a mortgage lender. There are several things that need to be taken into consideration here such as percent down, interest rate, and term or number of years to pay off.

## DOWN PAYMENT

Typically today a lender will want at least 30% down for all non-owner occupied properties. Anything less than this amount may subject you to Private Mortgage Insurance (PMI) which you do not want to pay. If you do have to pay this insurance, make sure it goes in the miscellaneous line under expenses, and make sure you multiply by 12 for the annual amount. Avoid PMI if at all possible, but if it is the only way to get the property then, by all means, consider it. If you plan to make improvements and can justify an increase in value to the property upon completion, you can ask and have the PMI waived. You will need another full appraisal to apply for this so you'll want to be right in your assessment of the proposed improvements.

# INTEREST RATES

The interest rates are all very low right now, but lenders are having a very hard time finding qualified borrowers since the Fed has tightened the requirements. This is one of the things that have been helping to keep the rates low. There is a lot of money available to lend, few borrowers to give it to. The interest rate you seek should be the lowest interest rate you can possible get.

Adjustable rate mortgages should not be considered under any circumstances when purchasing rental income property. There should never be a need so great that would entice you to place a wager on a future income stream. Having an adjustable mortgage jump by 2% points in a year can cost the owner an immense amount of trouble if they are unable to reduce other expenses and/ or raise income accordingly. I cannot stress enough to stay away from these.

# TERMS

Terms are the next area of consideration: number of years to repay. The term is the number of years upon which to make payments and in turn pay off the mortgage. There are different schools of thought in this matter, but the longer the term the better off you are from a cash flow perspective.

A 15 year payout will get you a slightly better interest rate, though you will be making higher payments since a greater amount is applied to the balance owed, the principal. It is not necessarily in your best interest to eliminate the loan more quickly. Remember, this is not your personal home, it is a business investment. Instead we will rely more on your personal needs and reasons for buying the property in the first place. Buying an income property when a child is born with a 15 year payoff is a great way to fund future college tuition. I know people who had purchased property as college funds and never needed to either sell or refinance the property to pay for college. They simply used the income generated monthly to pay tuition.

Personally. I like maximizing cash flow. Having a lower payment allows you to bank the difference and if there are vacancies, or unexpected needs arise, you are not locked into having a greater commitment than you need. Besides, you can always make extra payments when you have the cash. With a 15 year term, if you need more cash you won't be able to reduce the monthly payment you make though. Some things do not work reciprocally.

Points are the bank's way of taking advantage of uncertainty. They will offer you a reduction in the interest rate for, essentially, prepaying some of that interest up front in the way points. One point is 1% of the total value you are borrowing. If you are borrowing $150,000 then one point is $1,500 and for that you may be offered ¼% reduction in the interest rate. There are times I will pay these points and there are times I will not. If I intend to keep a property for a very long time I may pay a point or two to take advantage of a lower rate. If I suspect a rapid turn-around on the property I will not. Time creates the benefactor where points are concerned. Most mortgages never make it to the end before being paid off either through sale to another owner or refinanced for a multitude of reasons. Points have a break even factor, usually in terms of months or years. If paying a point will save me enough to recapture that point(s) in only a few years I may

> **Most mortgages never make it to the end before being paid off and points have a break even factor.**

take it. If it goes over 4 or 5 years to recover I will not. The bank is gambling on their being more financially savvy than you—don't forget what business the banks are in! The average holding period is considered by banks when they make these offers. If the banks did not usually make it out on top, they would not be offering points in the first place.

In order to get something populated in the Debt Service line I usually enter the asking price in the appropriate line below. It's as good a place to start as any. Using a 30% down payment will cause you the least grief from the lenders as well as avoid the PMI.

The Debt Service line should update automatically after entering the purchase price and the down payment percentage in the lines that follow. The amount is then adjusted by entering the term in number of years and the interest rate you will be paying. It is a good idea to sit with your personal banker before getting too involved looking at properties and meeting agents. Let them know what you are looking to do, see how you will be able to work together, and what you will qualify for. They will not be able to give you any kind of commitment since they need to see the leases and an income/expense report for the particular property in question, but you will get a general feel for your financial position. Do not flip through the newspaper and enter the fixed mortgage rate advertised that day. These rates are for owner occupied residential homes only, non-owner occupied income properties will always be a little higher.

# CASH FLOW BEFORE TAXES

This is the bottom line. Ideally there is a positive number in this line. Whatever number shows here will represent the amount left over after collecting all income and paying all bills—including your return on the investment money for down payment, closing costs, and upgrades. If there is a negative number it represents the amount of money you will have to put into the property on an annual basis in order to successfully operate the property.

The notion of "before taxes" is referring to the depreciation and the Schedule E for your personal tax return. This is not calculated as an investment line, but rather a perk. For larger properties and commercial assets it is a major consideration, but for what we are doing it is not. Please feel free to enjoy it though.

# CASH GENERATED ANNUALLY

The Cash Generated Annually is the sum total of the Owner's Return on Investment (from which you stated the interest rate you demand) and the Cash Flow Before Taxes.

# REPRESENTED ROI MADE

This is the represented rate of return; the interest rate you are receiving from the investment. Dollars received divided by the total dollars invested including down payment, closing costs, and improvements made.

# TAX SAVINGS

This entry is also a simple mathematical formula requiring only that you enter your current personal income tax rate. The figure has nothing to with valuating the property, but will give you a general idea of the amount of tax savings you can expect as a result of completing your schedule E from your other earned income.

Think back to chapter 3 to the investment comparisons where the government factor was introduced. The arrangement made by the US tax law as an incentive for you to purchase rental income property is the right to depreciate the value of the building (not the land) over a 30 year life expectancy. If the building you are purchasing is valued at $250,000 the building is estimated at 20% or $200,000 and the IRS allows this amount to be erased over 30 years. These amounts, percentages and durations change from year to year, so check with your tax preparer for the most current information. For example, $200,000 / 30 = $6,667 per year. This is the amount you would legally deduct your other earned income by, and thus, is the amount of reduction from your regular earned income which you will have to pay taxes on. If you earned $60,000 on your job and you claim a $6,667 reduction for depreciation on your Schedule E, you are only going to be responsible for paying regular income tax on $53,333 ($60,000 - $6,667). If you are in the 15% tax bracket then you are savings $1,000.05 in federal taxes ($6,667 x .15 = $1,000.15).

# TOTAL RETURN RECEIVED

This is the calculation of all monies to you, the investor. This includes the saving from your other earned income, the savings from depreciating this property based on the tax bracket and added to the ROI above.

# T O T A L   R O I

This is the rate of return generated by the above amount divided by the sum total of the investment being made. Provided your entries are researched and accurately entered, the Total ROI implies the equivalent interest rate returned from this investment. It is calculated by dividing the sum total of Owner's Return on Investment, Cash Flow Before Taxes and the Tax Savings Against Other Income by the Sum Total of the Down Payment, Closing Costs and Additional Cash Outlay.

$$\frac{\text{Owner's ROI} + \text{Cash Flow Before Taxes} + \text{Tax Savings Against Other Income}}{\text{Total of the Down Payment} + \text{Closing Costs} + \text{Additional Cash Outlay}} = \textbf{Total ROI}$$

This is also the rate you would have to generate from any of the other investments which could be made as alternatives to buying this property including stocks, bonds, and others.

Purchasing real estate is a time consuming and intensive process. It should therefore generate a worthy return in order to entice you to do it. If you find a building will generate an 8% ROI for only a $30,000 investment, I would take my chances with the stock market and save yourself the hassle. You want to be compensated justly for having endured the process. A 12% or better ROI is not an unrealistic target. However, in order to do that, sometimes things have to be manipulated. It is from here we are going to study some of the avenues that can be considered for manipulation. One particular property which was purchased a number of years ago best illustrates this point. We will explore all the variables that went into "making it work" by manipulating virtually everything.

CHAPTER TWELVE

# Spreadsheet Manipulation

At the risk of sounding repetitious, evaluating a property is not about finding a building you like. It is business! The fact of the matter is Column A has to hold a larger number than Column B when all final projections are made. It's the difference between "Red Ink" and "Being in the Black," between prosperity and bankruptcy. Only after the math tells you a building is a viable candidate should location and appearance be considered. Each aspect of the spreadsheet needs to be verified: the income, the expenses, the debt service options, everything. In essence, it boils down to you being a better businessman than the seller was, and about seeing more potential in the property than your competitors do.

In this chapter we are evaluating a property which was actually purchased when all the leading indicators initially told me this would never be the case. Manipulation of the numbers will tell the story regardless of the truths being hidden. Get the facts and let the math tell you what you need to know. In the end, as you will see, the hidden truth was the value the sellers could not see. Seen in the right light this is the proverbial story of not seeing the forest for the trees. And I never feel terribly obligated to tell a seller where he might be making a mistake.

Early in the process of examining this particular building I actually did walk away, but I was curious about the sheer oddity the numbers produced. Intrigued, I looked into it more as an exercise than anything else. I took the time to make a few calls and will retrace my steps from the initial discovery which began after seeing a sign on the property.

The building was a four-family unit a quarter mile from my residence and had been on the market for as long as I could remember. In fact I had looked into the property several years earlier and was told the seller would only be willing to sell if someone was willing to meet his price. The generally translated into a wealthy owner, someone who "… doesn't need the money, but will accept your offer if you're willing to pay his price." This anecdote was certainly not denied by the agent who suggested the property owner "… had no reason to move (on the price)."

My first mistake was believing that fable the first time around. Truth be told, I almost believed it the second time as well.

My initial inquiry had been about four years earlier—somewhere around 2003. The asking price of the building was higher than comparable properties in the area and it was not in good shape. It did not have a terrible appearance but was un-kept. It was not in a bad area either, it had an oversized lot and the most attractive quality to me was that the tenants paid all their own utilities including heat, hot water, and electric.

At the time I ran the numbers on the property I did not bother to look any further into it as I was told the seller was "very firm" on the price and there was no possible way the building would support the mortgage at the asking price. No tour of the inside was made, no offers were placed—I walked away.

Four years later this property again crossed my radar when I was sitting on my portion of the proceeds from the sale of the partnership and was in the market to replace that property. At first glance it seemed nothing had changed. Still for sale, same or close to the same price (I don't have the actual stats), and the same stubborn seller who was just as unmotivated and unwilling to negotiate.

Realtor.com was not as prominent then as it is today and I pulled the listing agent's name off the sign on the property and gave him a call. The initial inquiry (as discovered in 2007, there are no surviving records for the 2003 inquiry) was as shown in Table 12.1 below:

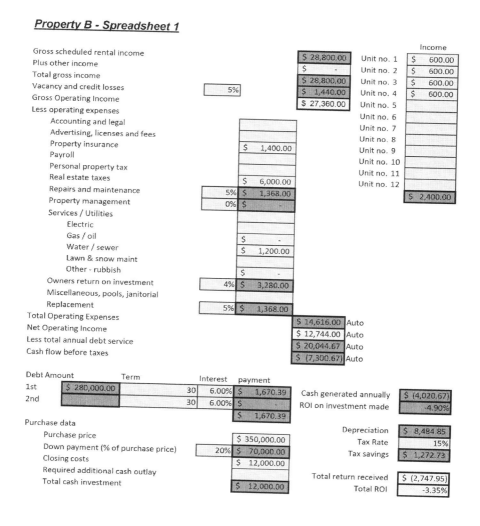

**Table 12.1 Property B—Spreadsheet 1**

The only data available was the amount of the rents, the insurance, water and taxes. This was the initial information entered onto the spreadsheet (plus the automatic percentages) and the results were rather dismal.

Once you begin verifying the figures you are given it rarely ever gets better for the bottom line. Sellers do not willingly tell you they pay for lawn maintenance, electric, or advertising, or anything they can remotely convince you they don't pay. Water bills do not end up as nice round numbers like $1,200 a year. I point this out to let you know that the numbers on the bottom line of the spreadsheet do not work and will only get worse, so why bother looking any deeper? Find another property. In this case the building would have had to have been purchased for exactly half the asking price in order to generate the return I demanded at the time. Look elsewhere is exactly what I did.

A month or two went by with no viable prospects on the map, when I stumbled across the listing again buried on my desk. Instead of just tossing it as I would normally have done, something caught my eye. The rent.

Believe it or not, more (small) income producing property is sold with the rents below the optimum level. This is mostly true of the small, part-time, non-professional landlord. This means the landlord has, for whatever reason, not raised the rents to the market value for the area the building is in. This may be due to fear of chasing tenants out, or he may just not want to be the bad guy. Whatever the reason your first obligation is to evaluate what the real rent projections are for the building based upon the average rents for the area where it is located and for the condition, size, and amenities offered. But this owner was not supposed to be the accidental landlord who received a property through the loss of a relative; it's what he did for a living.

The stated income for this particular property was woefully below the average for the area; hence oddity number one since he was quite aggressive in every aspect of the sale, especially in his asking price. A professional landlord would not allow his rent to be decidedly below any market, he would maximize the cash flow on all fronts. The little light bulb had just gone on and I filled out another spreadsheet. Plus, I was bored.

All the units were two-bedrooms and the tenants all paid their own natural gas and electric. At the time, a review of advertisements for two-bedroom apartments, I noted most were commanding rents between $900 and $1,000 per month, plus utilities.

I took a walk that evening past the building and noticed what I had not seen from the photos in the listing or my drive-by, the place was a dump. It was un-kept, garbage was strewn about, there was no off street parking, and it looked like an inner city condemnation candidate. But it also looked structurally sound. The roof line was straight, it had newly replaced windows and the vinyl siding was in good shape.

**The place was a dump ... but structurally sound with a straight roofline. Potential?**

It was clear the owner was not a professional, in fact he was anything but professional. My first inquiry thus became trying to understand why the rents were so far below the average. I simply took a plunge and added $100.00 to the expected rent for each apartment figuring that if I raised all the rents across the board, one tenant might leave and I could clean and upgrade that apartment allowing me to raise the rent by at least another $100.00 once completed. It would still be competitive enough to fill any vacancies quickly. Thus all apartments were raised on the spreadsheet to $700.00 from the original $600.00.

I went through the rest of the spreadsheet as well making assumptions as I went for each line item. What would I have to change to make this property work? I played with different scenarios as shown in Table 12.2.

This property does not sit on a busy thoroughfare and signs would not be visible to the mass population so the only way to rent the vacancies was through paid advertising. Regardless of the current owner's past practices this would be necessary in the future, so I added $280 per year for advertising costs.

A call to the tax assessor shed light on two things. First that the tax bill included a line for rubbish removal which we were told "was included in the tax bill," but was never added when the "taxes" were totaled. The taxes themselves were "rounded," ... so add another $122. The garbage added another $1,044 to the expense column.

A quick call to the insurance agent added another $327 in expenses.

The water and sewer bills the village clerk provided added another $434 to the ever-increasing expense column.

The village also has a landlord registry law in effect which cost $25 per apartment plus another $40 for each building per year that was forgotten. Add another annual $140 bill—this was not looking good.

We added $4,104 to the expenses of this building over what we were led to believe. Of this only $456 was our own doing occurring as an automatic increase when raising prospective rents from $600 to $700 and taking 5% of the net income for both repairs and replacement. The remaining $3,648 or 26% of the total presented expenses were from creative marketing, abject errors, and blatant omissions.

*Caveat emptor* ... "buyer beware."

## Property B - Spreadsheet 2

| | | | Income | |
|---|---|---|---|---|
| Gross scheduled rental income | | $ 33,600.00 | Unit no. 1 | $ 700.00 |
| Plus other income | | $ - | Unit no. 2 | $ 700.00 |
| Total gross income | | $ 33,600.00 | Unit no. 3 | $ 700.00 |
| Vacancy and credit losses | 5% | $ 1,680.00 | Unit no. 4 | $ 700.00 |
| Gross Operating Income | | $ 31,920.00 | Unit no. 5 | |
| Less operating expenses | | | Unit no. 6 | |
| Accounting and legal | | $ 140.00 | Unit no. 7 | |
| Advertising, licenses and fees | | $ 280.00 | Unit no. 8 | |
| Property insurance | | $ 1,727.00 | Unit no. 9 | |
| Payroll | | | Unit no. 10 | |
| Personal property tax | | | Unit no. 11 | |
| Real estate taxes | | $ 6,122.00 | Unit no. 12 | |
| Repairs and maintenance | 5% | $ 1,596.00 | | $ 2,800.00 |
| Property management | 0% | $ - | | |
| Services / Utilities | | | | |
| Electric | | | | |
| Gas / oil | | $ - | | |
| Water / sewer | | $ 1,634.00 | | |
| Lawn & snow maint | | | | |
| Other - rubbish | | $ 1,044.00 | | |
| Owners return on investment | 5% | $ 4,350.00 | | |
| Miscellaneous, pools, janitorial | | | | |
| Replacement | 5% | $ 1,596.00 | | |
| Total Operating Expenses | | $ 18,489.00 | Auto | |
| Net Operating Income | | $ 13,431.00 | Auto | |
| Less total annual debt service | | $ 20,044.67 | Auto | |
| Cash flow before taxes | | $ (6,613.67) | Auto | |

| Debt | Amount | Term | Interest | payment | | |
|---|---|---|---|---|---|---|
| 1st | $ 280,000.00 | 30 | 6.00% | $ 1,670.39 | Cash generated annually | $ (2,263.67) |
| 2nd | | 30 | 6.00% | $ - | ROI on investment made | -2.60% |
| | | | | $ 1,670.39 | | |

| Purchase data | | | |
|---|---|---|---|
| Purchase price | $ 350,000.00 | Depreciation | $ 8,484.85 |
| Down payment (% of purchase price) | 20% $ 70,000.00 | Tax Rate | 15% |
| Closing costs | $ 12,000.00 | Tax savings | $ 1,272.73 |
| Required additional cash outlay | $ 5,000.00 | Total return received | $ (990.95) |
| Total cash investment | $ 17,000.00 | Total ROI | -1.14% |

## Table 12.2 Property B—Spreadsheet 2

About now you the see pattern emerging, it is not your imagination. We added 17% across the board to all the rents and we still showed a loss every year. Sellers all do this with their numbers and I don't know why. It is not like a buyer will not figure it out, we will. If we miss something our attorney will not. If you don't ask, you may never know. Well that is not entirely true, you will find out shortly after you sign the closing documents.

Nothing I had uncovered made any sense. It is not always enough to look at things through your own eyes. The world is skewed to your prejudices and so every once in a while it is best to look at the emerging picture through the eyes of the current owner. In this case the owner had this particular property for a little over 8 years. Shortly after he bought it, he placed it for sale at a higher price. That also means he had only owned it for perhaps a couple of years when I first inquired in 2003.

He had a mortgage on the property in the amount of roughly $156,000 and since this mortgage was about 8 years old in 2007, I calculated the interest rate at about 7-1/2%. When I worked the accurate numbers I had for the taxes and garbage (he may have been paying less for insurance so I used his) into the spreadsheet I found he was still making $2,700 a year. This is by no means accurate but, it does show why he was selling the property. If the current ROI of a hundred thousand dollars in the bank is worth more than the income generated by the property with that equity, it is time to liquidate, or refinance. I made a mental note to remember this later, but it still didn't answer the question of why. This property should have been producing a much higher return and now I was determined to find out what was wrong. Table 12.3 shows what I perceived as the owner's correct situation.

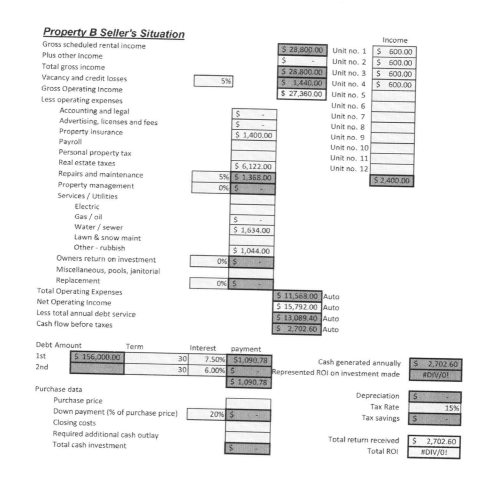

### Property B Seller's Situation

| | | | | | | Income | |
|---|---|---|---|---|---|---|---|
| Gross scheduled rental income | | | $ 28,800.00 | Unit no. 1 | $ 600.00 |
| Plus other income | | | $ - | Unit no. 2 | $ 600.00 |
| Total gross income | | | $ 28,800.00 | Unit no. 3 | $ 600.00 |
| Vacancy and credit losses | 5% | | $ 1,440.00 | Unit no. 4 | $ 600.00 |
| Gross Operating Income | | | $ 27,360.00 | Unit no. 5 | |
| Less operating expenses | | | | Unit no. 6 | |
| Accounting and legal | | $ - | | Unit no. 7 | |
| Advertising, licenses and fees | | $ - | | Unit no. 8 | |
| Property insurance | | $ 1,400.00 | | Unit no. 9 | |
| Payroll | | | | Unit no. 10 | |
| Personal property tax | | | | Unit no. 11 | |
| Real estate taxes | | $ 6,122.00 | | Unit no. 12 | |
| Repairs and maintenance | 5% | $ 1,368.00 | | | | $ 2,400.00 |
| Property management | 0% | $ - | | | | |
| Services / Utilities | | | | | | |
| Electric | | | | | | |
| Gas / oil | | $ - | | | | |
| Water / sewer | | $ 1,634.00 | | | | |
| Lawn & snow maint | | | | | | |
| Other - rubbish | | $ 1,044.00 | | | | |
| Owners return on investment | 0% | $ - | | | | |
| Miscellaneous, pools, janitorial | | | | | | |
| Replacement | 0% | $ - | | | | |
| Total Operating Expenses | | | $ 11,568.00 | Auto | | |
| Net Operating Income | | | $ 15,792.00 | Auto | | |
| Less total annual debt service | | | $ 13,089.40 | Auto | | |
| Cash flow before taxes | | | $ 2,702.60 | Auto | | |

| Debt Amount | | Term | | Interest | payment | | |
|---|---|---|---|---|---|---|---|
| 1st | $ 156,000.00 | | 30 | 7.50% | $1,090.78 | Cash generated annually | $ 2,702.60 |
| 2nd | | | 30 | 6.00% | $ - | Represented ROI on investment made | #DIV/0! |
| | | | | | $ 1,090.78 | | |

| Purchase data | | | | |
|---|---|---|---|---|
| Purchase price | | | Depreciation | $ |
| Down payment (% of purchase price) | 20% | $ - | Tax Rate | 15% |
| Closing costs | | | Tax savings | $ - |
| Required additional cash outlay | | | | |
| Total cash investment | | $ - | Total return received | $ 2,702.60 |
| | | | Total ROI | #DIV/0! |

## Table 12. 3 Property B—Seller's Situation

Utility bills can be fascinating. This is always true when the landlord is responsible for paying the heat, but this was not the case here since the tenants paid their own. Because this was a four-family building and there were only four electric meters, someone had to be paying for the electric usage for the basement, hallway, and outdoor lighting that the landlord should be responsible for. This, albeit not a major issue, was not disclosed.

There were gas meters for each of the four apartments in this building as well. This was good news as it was a clear indicator that the tenants were not just dividing up the expenses as they came in. Each tenant was clearly responsible for their own gas and electric. We were told during the initial inquiry that each tenant paid for their own hot water, cooking gas, electricity and heat which is the ideal situation for a residential property. We found this to be true.

And during this investigation, we also found the smoking gun.

We were told the heating bills each tenant paid was relatively high, typically $600 per apartment. I knew based on my own personal experience that the utility company for the area this building was located in bills every other month. Thus, $300 per month for combined gas and electric raised enough concern to look deeper into it. The tenants could not be expected to pay more rent if their utility bills were eating too large a piece of their total housing allowance. Budgeting or not, everyone knows how much they can afford to pay each month. After asking about the insulation and windows and other typical "Why are the heating bills so high?" questions it came out that the heat was not taking advantage of that nice clean efficient natural gas, but was in fact, electric. Electric heat is always more costly and less efficient than gas, so the bills were no longer that big of a surprise. However, nothing that man can get himself involved in is ever so ridiculous or inept that adding a little stupidity cannot make it at least a little bit worse.

These tenants were not billed every other month, they were billed every single month. The bills they paid were not $600 every two months it was $600 every month during the heating season. They were paying as much for the heat as they were for their rent! The utility company changed their modus operandi and began billing every month after the installation of the new heating systems. It was then disclosed that the source of heat being electric was not the problem but the medium of the delivery was. The owners, to find the cheapest route of fixing a failed heating system had installed electric radiant heating coils in the ceilings.

Heat rises.

Radiant heat is a beautiful thing, but not in the ceilings. Heating the ceilings and expecting that heat to warm the floors is about as backward as it can get. During the winter heating season—which can run from October to March or exactly half the year—these tenants were paying just as much for heating their apartments as they were for renting their apartments and the sum total of the two was above the area average housing allowance.

Under the financial constraints these tenants were living we would not be able to raise the rents, nor would we ever keep tenants in the building. I pictured a mass exodus every September. Indeed all the tenants except one had moved into the building in the course of the past year. Turnover was huge. But even worse was that the tenants were told the same thing as I was, that the company billed every other month. The tenants were all surprised when in December of every year they had to start looking for a place to live or risk damaging their credit trying to pay the bills. The landlord was shrewd to have the security deposits. Nobody ever moved in winter as they all signed year-long leases so the landlord never had to pay the heat on a vacant unit to keep the pipes from freezing. Not that he would have.

The numbers that were presented here were so far off the trail of financial solvency that under any normal circumstances we were now completely and utterly done, but I was still very curious about a couple of things. I decided to go the distance on a hunch I suspect as more of an educational exercise than an actual purchase consideration plan.

The perplexing question at this particular point in time became not how this building got itself into such a financially precarious position as it did, but if anything could be done to get it out, and what that might take.

People know how much they are willing to spend for housing costs. You can push the envelope a bit here and there with amenities and niceties, but not much. In this area the going housing expense average hovers around $1,200 a month which this building was already at. So the question became what could be done not to increase this total amount but rather to sway where this money goes. If the rental market was $1,200 per month and $600 of that was going to places it need not be going, was there a viable option that intellect could fix?

**Heating costs had handcuffed this property.**

Heating costs had handcuffed this property and the only way to know whether anything was possible in this regard was to go the next step and make an official visit to the property as a prospective buyer.

I scratched my head for a while over this, but in the end made a call to an architect and asked him to accompany me during a walkthrough of the property. The purpose was to evaluate the possibility of installing high efficiency gas fired heating systems, and to consider what possible delivery methods these new units might have, i.e., hot water baseboard, forced hot air etc. He agreed and suggested we add the task of measuring out the building to show walls, doors, windows, stairs, and all other major components. This is known as establishing existing conditions, which would allow easier design parameters later if we got that far. I did not want to shell out anything more than necessary, but allowed him to convince me to take the measurements. He would not draft anything unless and until it should proceed further. For $200 he agreed, drafting the existing condition drawings would be another $1,000 at a later date. Not even this was to happen until I had done a very brief, representative walk though myself first.

I called the realtor back and set up an appointment to see if I could convince myself that the idea could have enough merit in my own eyes to pursue any further. The realtor set up a quick tour accessing two of the four apartments for that afternoon.

My initial summation was very positive as all of the apartments were the same. The building was divided into two floors with mirror image apartments on each side and the second floor was the same as the first. In other words they were stacked, bathrooms over bathrooms, kitchens over kitchens, which saves on piping and eliminates other problems. Furthermore it had a full basement and enough attic space to crawl though for utility lines and such. The building was about 80 years old and was originally built as a tavern on the first floor and rooms for rent on the second. The apartments were all flats meaning you walked though rooms to get to other rooms and so on, not ideal and were in very poor condition.

There is an overused cliché in real estate everyone has heard of, location, location, location which I suggest, is not true. There is much more to it than that. For this reason I developed a weighted scorecard to rate a potential building. I will tell you up front I do not use this as you see it here on a sheet of paper, but I do use it in my head when walking potential properties. In other words, I have looked at so many properties by now I instinctively know what I do and what I do not like to see. But I reprinted it here for you to use until a level of comfort develops.

The weights are as follows:

- ◌ 25% Numbers
- ◌ 25% Architectural Considerations
- ◌ 20% Location
- ◌ 15% Condition
- ◌ 15% Marketability.

First of all how could the rule of location, location, location possibly apply when so much of this country is already developed? Everywhere you look, somebody found that great location, location, location!

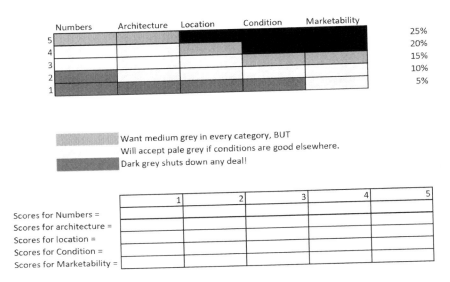

**Table 12.4 Weighted Scorecard**

Minimum scores should be added as well as some categories should not be permitted to have low scores. e.g., For example, Condition can be allowed to be a low score as it will have other effects such as reduction in offering price to compensate for the rehabilitation expense, but serious architectural issues cannot be addressed if the structure cannot be easily changed.

By and far the Numbers category should be completed first. If the numbers do not generate the desired ROI then going through the rest of the process is moot, good for practice only. Once again, never allow yourself to fall in love with a property.

The next most important category to be considered is the Architectural Features. Are the apartments arranged in such a fashion that requires passage from a bedroom through another bedroom to get to the bath? Is the bathroom door next to the dining room table? There are certain things that are extremely difficult and cost prohibitive to overcome. A chief concern to consider is sound attenuation between the apartments. Sounds emanating between apartments can be extremely distressing to the occupants and is, in my opinion, one of the most frequent reasons for building owners putting their buildings on the market in the first place. Tenants with sound problems often don't get along, though they don't always know what the root cause to their complaints are. Sound issues cause high turnover and that is very costly. If I am still interested because the numbers have worked out (category #1), then this is my next highest reason for walking away from a deal after category #2—Architectural Considerations. These are the things I focus on during my initial visits. Logically, I should have already been out the door on this property. The numbers didn't work, so ordinarily I would have walked away. Architecturally is was not great either. By now it was intrigue that kept my interest.

I called the architect back after my initial visit and explained what I had found. With this information he suggested a couple of approaches. Since there was a full basement and a crawl space attic he suggested gas fired hot air burners. The duct work would be minimal and I could add central air-conditioning to further increase the value to the tenants. An amenity. He thought the cost to be in the $7,000 per unit range. With this we collectively scheduled a formal site visit.

I set up the appointment with the architect for the following week and used the architect as the home inspector.

# HOME INSPECTION

I do not personally use home inspection reports for buildings I buy unless required to do so by the bank. I do my own evaluations and I look for things by category including structural, mechanical and electrical integrity. Plumbing I include as a part of mechanical. If I find something within a certain category I don't like I will call in an expert in that category. I do this because it will serve two purposes. If, as was the case in this situation, I questioned the lack of an electrical meter for the common area lighting, it was easy enough to have my electrician show up at the same time to evaluate the service panels and give me a quote to fix the problem rather than making a third appointment. The realtor was surprised to see him show up but since he did not have to access any of the apartments there was a simple apology and we moved on. I am old school and believe in the old adage it is easier to ask forgiveness than it is to ask permission. Besides, I don't like to scare tenants more frequently than I have to.

Home inspections are valuable investments to make if you are not sure about the things to look for. I highly recommend having home inspections done if you are anything less than an expert yourself and in a lot of cases today, lenders will require them anyway. Some home sellers are having inspections completed in advance and copies presented to the potential buyers, but credibility has come into question as a conflict of interest issue. Who paid for the inspection?

During the official walk through the architect and I measured the rooms, the building perimeter, the window and door locations and sizes, fixtures, appliances, everything. He spent time in the attic recording structure framing sizes, direction and length of spans. He recorded insulation and identified major heat loss areas. He recorded the locations and structural issues in the basement, foundation opening, gas and electrical meters, water main size and location. When complete he went to his office and drafted the floor plans, elevations and a cross section of the building as it existed that day.

During this process he discovered another anomaly. It would appear that the owners of the building had taken extreme steps to save money on general maintenance of their building. The cross section he had drawn was missing 12" of vertical space. The floor to floor height he had measured in the common area hallway from the finished first floor to the finished second floor was 9 feet 11 inches. But the finished ceiling in all four apartments was only 8 feet. By all calculations the finished ceiling of the first floor apartments was 23" below the finished floor of the apartments above them.

I spent a little bit more than I would have for a home inspection report but this might never have come up. The apartments seemed to be quiet but this revealed why. When the sellers had looked for the least expensive way to replace the heating system they had lowered the ceiling with separate ceiling framing, installed a layer of 3/8" sheetrock, put up a layer of joint compound with the heat coils embedded in it and covered the still wet joint compound with another layer of 3/8" sheet rock. On top of this new construction they had 6" of blown in insulation added.

# DIAMOND IN THE ROUGH

You could march a herd of elephants across the floors upstairs and never hear it below. This was the second glimmer of good news.

The floor plan layout was terrible. You had to walk through bedrooms to get to kitchens and bathrooms and there no rationale for how the walls were laid out. It was typical 1950s era design. This was the estimated timeframe the building was converted from single rooms to actual apartments. Again it was the least expensive route possible, but even this suggested good news. If the partitions were not original to the framing, then they could be moved without affecting the structural integrity of the overall building.

The building all of a sudden began to take on the look of a severely mismanaged gem, a proverbial and potential "diamond in the rough." My interest in this building was increasing, but there was more to consider. For example, part of the Architectural Considerations category takes into account the safety of the tenants.

Appliances that don't work, electrical shorts and overloaded circuits, missing ground faults, missing electrical covers, broken glass, doors that don't close properly, leaking fixtures, and leaks in general are sought, the overall condition of the water supply and sewer lines ... and on and on. Throughout the inspection process I look for any and all potential safety issues, and this property was no different.

Next I looked for things like sagging framing and beams, failing concrete in the foundation and evidence of water on the basement floor. How does the roof look, gutters and leaders, where do they drain to, what is the parking situation, is there enough for all the tenants and their guests? This particular building had it all. Water was evident in the basement up to a depth of six inches. There was no parking lot at all and the tenants were all forced to find their own parking in the winter months as the village did not allow on street parking during snow storms. There were leaks of every kind, both water and sewer. There was no drainage from rain water leaders, just straight drops to the foundation walls where it readily seeped into and up through the basement floor.

There were *lots* of problems, but there were no serious structural problems and all of issues could be eliminated. It had a certificate of occupancy as a legal four family. The building sat on the far side of large village lot that readily allowed a parking lot to be built, it had all stacked kitchens and baths, allowing the complete replacement of water and sewer lines without a massive degree of retrofit. Access through either of the two first floor apartments would allow us to completely replace the water and sewer lines in all four unit's bathrooms and kitchens.

The equation was beginning to balance in my head—more importantly, in my gut.

It was worth taking another hard look at the numbers to see what might be possible. In the next spreadsheet notice a lowered asking price. I decided the truth was somewhat obscure and that I would not go above $315k as a final price knowing what I learned. We had also decided that since the bathrooms were all stacked and back to back, as were the kitchens, we would install separate water meters as well. Rents were brought up to where they could be once the burden of the radiant heating was eliminated and central air-conditioning was to be installed as a perk. See Table 12.5 below:

### Property B - Spreadsheet 3

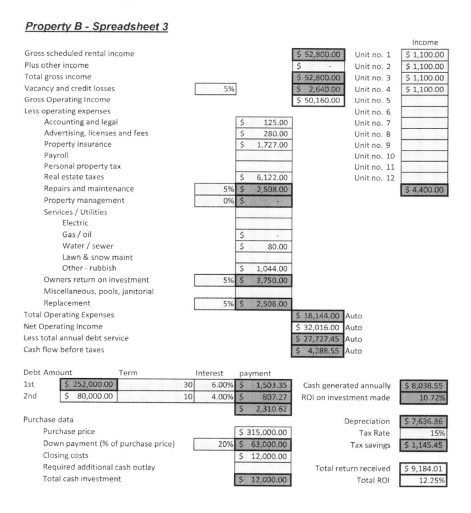

**Table 12.5 Property B—Spreadsheet 3**

What this plan did was increase the Net Income line from $31,920 to $50,160 and remove $1,554 in water bills that the tenants would now be paying. The overall increase to the Net Operating Income was the most dramatic going from $13,431 to $32,016 a whopping 134% increase.

The only thing left to do was to decide on the details of an offer to be submitted and for how much. We initially offered $285k, countered back and forth for a few days and were stalemated at my offer of $310k to his $325k. I offered $315K as a final. The seller came down to $320k and I walked away. About two weeks later he called agreeing to the $315k and we signed the contracts.

# RETURN ON RENOVATION

While the closing was being prepared we were busy preparing for the changes to come. Plans were drafted for the new layout of the apartments. The plans converted the apartments from flats to a new open floor plan look, island kitchens with eat at counters and all new appliances, gas stoves, microwave range hoods, ice maker refrigerators and dishwashers were planned for each apartment. The heating systems proved to be even easier than the architect and I had anticipated. The installer asked about putting the second floor heating units on the second floor eliminating lengthy supply and return trunk lines and increasing the efficiency even more. A small room was built on the second floor landing that had previously been an unsightly and unauthorized makeshift tenant storage space for bicycles and baby strollers.

Quotes were gathered from several contractors for various aspects of the work and an estimate for the total transformation of a building had begun. The best news though came from an agreement between the architect and the heating contractor when they agreed the ducting and vents could be placed now and made operational and would not have to be altered when the new floor plans were built. I would be able to immediately install the units, minimize tenant utility bills and be able to capture most of that coveted monthly housing allowance for myself.

This spreadsheet looks a bit different from the previous one as there is now a second line for the cost of renovations under the debt service category. It was determined that borrowing $80k from an equity line source at 4% for 10 years could provide the funding required as long as the income line would support both the new proposed first mortgage as well as the equity line. The equity line was on the home we live in and not the property being purchased.

We studied the rental market very closely and determined that very nice, essentially new 2 bedroom apartments with well appointed kitchens, high efficiency gas fired direct vent heating and air conditioning would rent at $1,100 per month allowing $100 per month for utility bills.

We combined efforts in several areas since it was necessary to have a driveway installed which required the removal of 5 large trees and considerable earth movement. We had that contractor install subterranean piping for rain water removal, a trench for the plumber to install a new 2-1/2" water main and new concrete curb cut at the road and re-grade the front and sides of the property for greater water drainage.

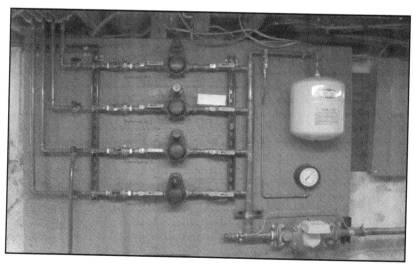

The plumber replaced 100% of the sewer line from the connection at the basement wall and installed 5 new water meters, replaced all plumbing in the house with new plastic with a manifold setup in the basement for each connection in the building. This allows for easy maintenance since if there is a leak on either hot or cold side of any water faucet of any apartment it could be shut off from the basement without affecting any other water in that apartment or building.

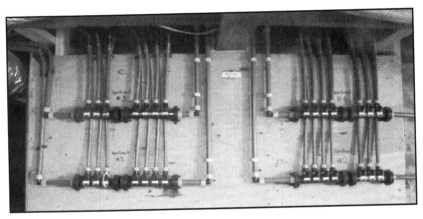

None of these were considered by the tax assessor to be improvements. This was important as the taxes would have gone up if they had been. Parking was the questionable item as there had been no parking previously. We were told, "Well, there should have been parking …" and they let it slide. Everything else was simply altering what was already there. There was heat in the building before and there still is was the rationale. We would not add any square footage to the building, we just rearranged what it already had.

I added another spreadsheet, showing income and expenses through 2 years after closing and having completed 90% of the renovations laid out. As I write this, one of the apartments has still not been retrofitted with a new layout as the original tenants are still there. The heat and AC and safety issues have all been corrected in that unit, but the floor plan has not been updated for this last remaining apartment. If I figure out how to do it with the tenants still in the building I will, otherwise it will be done once they leave or take a vacation for at least two weeks.

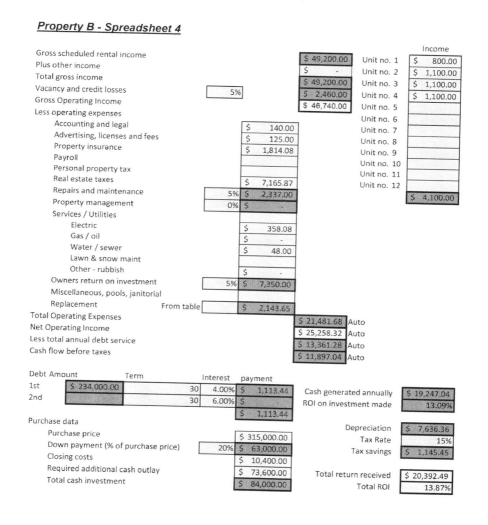

**Table 12.6 Property B—Spreadsheet 4**

This last spreadsheet tells the story best as it means that exploring, curiosity, and careful manipulation of things can pay off. You can see some differences right away as we did not spend the total anticipated amounts on the reconstruction. The last apartment will eventually cost about $10,000. Another change was that we did not assign the equity payments to the building but simply make these from the overall ROI, the income will allow all of the construction costs to be completely repaid in less than 4 years. The other thing that happened was taking care of the mortgage company. Due to the severe housing market meltdown and after being reduced in value, this building is sitting comfortably with a 47% equity position today which was confirmed by a full appraisal since, after completing this work, it was refinanced reducing the interest rate to 4.0% fixed for 30 years. Remember, it was purchased right at the beginning of the housing bust, before losing some 30% of its perceived value. When the market recovers completely, it could be worth a half million.

Strictly from the perspective of an investment, I can get a return from a money market account today of at best 2%. If I were even able to find an investment that would pay me 6%, I would have to place $324,000 in that investment to get the $19,247.00 this investment generates. I never had more than $147,700 in this investment at any time. The time I put into this property now is about 5 hours a month. How many hours a year will the average person work to earn $19,247.00?

Normally, only the math should suggest either looking at a property or discarding it out of hand. In the end it was still the math that made this possible, we just had to be more creative when crunching the numbers. It was the worst case example I had to show how various aspects of things can be taken into consideration. This building sits comfortably in my portfolio today and undoubtedly will for quite some time. It took a bit of work and a lot of thinking outside the box. That's my point: I am not Donald Trump, not the quintessential expert. I am a blue-collar working man who made the necessary calls and put this and other things together. I am proud of that and know beyond the shadow of a doubt that if I can do this you can do it as well.

CHAPTER THIRTEEN

# The Art of Negotiation

There are many books on the art of negotiation. Read as many as you can. Robert Allen's *Nothing Down* focuses on the multitude of ways to purchase a piece of real estate. This is a great guide for the possibilities you could encounter. Still, like snowflakes, no two purchases are ever the same.

You've run the numbers, reviewed the property, met with the tenants, and taken lots of notes, but what do you really know? If you've done all things correctly about the building, the tenants, and the profit and loss sheets, you should know a lot. But what do you know about the sellers? It is entirely possible to make it this far without even meeting the sellers, but that should not mean you do not know them. Sometimes a purchase is made in which the purchasers and the sellers never meet, never even speak. Such are the possibilities within the mechanisms that drive our legal system today. So how do you find the sellers' motivations, their intentions and their desires? Do they matter? Should you even care about the sellers? You're not adopting a child from them, you simply want a physical possession which currently belongs to them. So is it worth trying to "get into their heads" and see what they are all about? I would have to say yes.

In the case of the 4-family building in the last chapter, according to the realtor, I should have paid that "firm price" he so emphatically pushed. So let's say I did. I would have been out an additional $7,000 in down payment, my mortgage would have risen by $104.04 per month, my annual cash flow would have been reduced by $1,877.20 and my ROI reduced from 12.25% to 8.91%. Closing costs would have been higher as well, but you get the picture. Yes, it pays to get into their heads. They are trying to get into yours, and for the same reasons. Play poker, act disinterested. Don't try to "buy their building," make them try to "sell you their building."

> ## Don't try to "buy their building," make them try to "sell you their building."

If you think back to the property in the last chapter there were several indications presented that suggested the sellers were not what they claimed to be. Paying attention will come in handy should you actually get into negotiations. If needed, I am not afraid to come right out and tell the sellers to their face how much of a return they are really making (not what they say they are making) and how much cash their sale to me will generate. They will always tell you your calculations are all wrong, but that's okay, they are attempting to play poker as well. Internally they are salivating all over your alleged errors. Do not show any excitement.

The first clue that I knew little about negotiating came at the closing table on our very first purchase, an owner occupied three-family building. One tenant was the seller's daughter and the only tenant paying rent was a close family friend of hers. I know the family friend didn't bother to pay rent and I suspect the father never pursued rent from his offspring either. Effectively, he was subsidizing everyone in the building on his rather sparse retirement. He was not covering his costs and he was not enjoying his retirement

We went through all the normal investigations, inspections, qualifying and so-on and made an offer to buy to buy the building. (This building would not have received a passing score on my spreadsheet today.)

In the end we opted for a VA loan since this was my first purchase and the VA was available and I didn't know any better. In the contracts the seller's attorneys had stated the sellers would pay the 4 points required for a VA 30 year mortgage. However, during the contract negotiations rates came down and we opted to pursue a 15 year mortgage, as I said I was young and made mistakes. A fifteen-year VA mortgage required 6 points to be paid. The VA required "the points" to be paid by "the seller." They assumed they were on the hook for $2,000, 4% of $50,000 not 6% which would be $3,000. Our attorney saw the train wreck ahead and added to the contract rider a rather simple and innocuous little statement "…seller shall pay points…" This went unchallenged since they had already agreed to pay the 4 points up front, there was no dispute. The rider was signed and as such, superseded the signed contracts.

At the closing table I had no idea what everyone was screaming about and when it was explained to me by the seller's attorney I offered up a bunch of ways to make it right. I was literally dragged out of the bank by my attorney and told to shut up and stay out of it!

Say what?!

This was my first property and it represented my future. Hell no I won't stay out of it! I wanted this deal to go through and he was not about to screw it up. I offered something to the seller under the table to ensure they would not walk away.

In the end, our attorney knew full well what I did not. That there was no way these sellers would ever walk away from that table. We represented cash. We represented an end to his misery. We represented the only viable alternative to a deadbeat child and the subsidizing of friends thereof. It might have been several thousand dollars more but no, he was not going to leave that table. My attorney sat there stone cold and indignant completely ignoring the sweat rolling off my forehead. I hated him in advance for costing me this deal. Then, with no victory celebration at all, the sellers—to my utter shock—capitulated and 5 minutes later the deal was closed, the under the table deal null and void, and I was a home owner.

I learned more in 30 minutes that day than in any 30 day period in my life before or after. And I desperately wanted to know how my attorney could be so confident.

## WHEN TO GIVE, WHEN TO HOLD FIRM

Negotiating is indeed an art. No question about it. But how do you know what to base negotiations on? Knowing what to give up and when to push for your demands is great knowledge to have. Learn everything you can to improve these skills. In the end you have to have the knowledge of the needs of your adversary and you have to solve their problems. Ulterior motives may develop as you gain the upper hand on information. This information is critical to the understanding of the real reasons the sellers are trying to sell in the first place. Maybe they want to raise the capital for a 1031 exchange; if they have the property in mind they may be motivated. They may simply want to be retire and don't care how long it takes to liquidate and can afford to wait for the right price. But finding the truth behind their motivations allows you to customize the deal to solve "their" problems to "your" distinct advantage. In doing so, you will sweeten the deal considerably for yourself. Your purpose is to negotiate the best deal, lowest price, lowest rate, longest term, furthest balloon, most ancillary articles included etc. Your own ulterior motives are kept close to the chest.

One good example of how this can be beneficial to you as a buyer was in 1985 when we stumbled upon a small ramshackle 2 family building in dire need of everything. It was in a nice city location with valuable off-street parking and directly across from a beautiful park. During the vetting process, we learned the sellers were physically afraid of the tenants they had rented the property to—very afraid. Armed with this information and the fact the building was in terrible shape, we asked for a substantial discount for a cash purchase "as-is." They countered with a higher price and we walked away. Two weeks went by before the phone rang, but it did ring. The two weeks subdued the sellers completely as no one else was willing to tackle it and another first of the month had passed without any income from the tenants. We stipulated to the sellers' attorneys we would close on the building only after the city building department condemned the property, effectively forcing the existing tenants out ... making the city be the bad guys. They quickly agreed since the sellers were too frightened to attempt to evict them themselves. We paid a reduced price of $33,000 down from an original $57,000 asking price. This was an all cash purchase since no bank was remotely willing to finance it. Once we had possession we filed for a building permit to convert the property from two 3 (tiny) bedrooms per unit to two upscale 2-bedroom units.

The mechanical systems were all entirely replaced and the floor plans were rearranged which required several minor structural changes as well. In the end we had spent over the course of 5 months $27,000 and managed to line up good tenants who moved in immediately upon issuance of the certificate of occupancy. This was followed right away by a new first position mortgage based on a "new" current appraised value. The bank appraised the property at $90,000 and we took a $60,000 first mortgage effectively giving us a completely rebuilt 2 family building for free. The first month the mortgage payment was made we generated a positive cash flow and it has done so every month since except those few months where we had vacancies.

# SOLVE THE PROBLEM AND WIN

Now in this example the information was up front and we were able to solve the sellers' real issue in a fashion that was very lucrative for ourselves in the form of a greatly reduced price. Many people had looked at this property, but no offer had been entertained because all required the sellers to take action in evicting the tenants from the premises. Allowing a willing third party to force them out was an exit strategy not previously considered. This is the advantage knowledge allows. But the knowledge need not be your own.

I was not the one who thought of having the building condemned as a means of extracting the problems within. I had explained in detail what our intentions with the building were and credit for the condemnation goes to my attorney (not the same attorney in the earlier example). However, it was I who learned the real nature of the sellers' problem and had the wherewithal to ask my attorney for suggestions.

I've negotiated a lot of deals since then. I have read a lot of books and I have refined my abilities. There's an old saying I like: "After birth, death is inevitable, everything else is negotiable." This is absolutely true. In real estate, everyone knows price is negotiable. But everything else should not be overlooked.

Probably the best example of this I have ever done was in negotiating the purchase of a vacant twelve acre lot we bought to build a new residence for ourselves. The property was listed with a realtor after having given up trying to sell on his own. He had recently retired and was doing well financially. He had subdivided the property years earlier and this was the last remaining parcel he had to liquidate, his business which sat on one of the adjacent parcels had sold the year before. He had 4 grown children and they were all out of the area and had no interest in the land. All this information was freely presented by the realtor during an hour long conversation. I walked the property formulating an offer.

The asking price was $46,000 and the appraised value was $55,000. It had been for sale by owner for $49,000. Most people who try to sell property on their own are doing so in order to squeeze every dollar possible for themselves. If they change their minds and list with a realtor, they often raise the price to cover the cost of the commission they now have to pay. This one signed on with a realtor and had dropped the price. This suggested the money was not the most important part of the equation. I spoke to the realtor and let him know my intention was to build a home in which I would raise my family and this was conveyed to the seller who seemed content we were not looking to subdivide or otherwise "mess up his property." This indicated pride was a factor in the equation as well.

We had initially intended to pay cash for the property from an account we had been building, but this information changed the playing field dramatically. We put a low ball offer on the property with four parameters designed to encourage countering and get a more accurate feel for the seller. The offer was for the purchase price of $35,000 with 10% down and the balance over 30 years at 6% interest to the seller directly. We knew this was not going to be accepted and the realtor told us there was no chance of his ever accepting only 10% down and argued vehemently against our putting the offer in as written, but we insisted. The first real surprise for me came in the fact that there was a counter offer at all. Additionally, the seller completely stunned the realtor stating he had no problem with the 10% down. This was not quite as surprising to me and reinforced my notion of having accurately assumed his financial state.

He further countered that the price he needed to have would be $45,000 and that he would be willing to take a note but for only 10 years. The interest rate would have to be 10%. This was a great start! We countered his offer immediately saying we would oblige the 10 year payout <u>he wanted</u>, and we would pay the 10% interest rate <u>he wanted</u> as well. Further we confirmed our intent and offered to keep the same $4,500 as the down payment <u>he wanted</u> but in meeting these terms <u>for him</u> we could not pay more than $37,000 for the property and that we sincerely hoped he could understand. He once again countered. He had accepted the $37,000 purchase price and the down payment, but only on the condition we paid the note at an interest rate of 12% and amortized over 8 years. We immediately agreed to all.

Our attorney placed a clause in the rider to the contract eliminating any pre-payment penalty which was accepted with little argument with the understanding that when we started to build we would not be able to get a first mortgage with an existing loan on the property. There was a lengthy closing preparation (there were 2 legal issues to resolve prior to our taking possession) we closed in the middle of November—the original offer was made in late April. The first payment was due on December 1 which we made. Then, on the 27th of December of that same year we called the seller and asked for the payoff amount on the note informing him of our intention to pay it off before the first of the year. We had only made one mortgage payment at 12%. His complete reaction was "Oh, very smooth." We had the property appraised in the spring of the following year after having had possession of it for only 4 months at $87,000 and it was free and clear.

Now, one more thing to discuss under the fine art of negotiating, I like to sleep well at night. Nowhere in any of these negotiations can I be described as a liar with perhaps the exception where I told this last seller "...we could not pay more than $37,000 for the property." This was not a lie, it was simply part of the negotiation process. I did my homework in finding out as much as I could about that seller. I am also an open book and had he taken the time to understand me, the outcome could have been considerably different, but that is simply how that hand was played out. Another famous quote pertaining to real estate, is "All sellers are liars; all buyers are thieves." I leave that to the debate teams. What is true though, is that knowledge is power. And knowledge is the most important asset you can ever have on your side in the negotiating process.

> **Knowledge is the most important asset in the negotiating process.**

Sometimes though, negotiating is not necessary. Sometimes a deal can come to you that suggests honesty and integrity in the sellers. When this happens you simply have to act. Some people, not in the business, really believe "deals to-good-to-be-true," **don't** actually exist, but they do. You just have to recognize them and be ready to act when they come along. The only way to recognize them is to understand them.

A completely different scenario presented itself as a very well cared for little single family home on a dead end street in a beautiful blue collar neighborhood. It had a fenced yard, full and dry basement, patio with a stone grill, and lot's more. The ad said "2-bedroom, $50,000, $10,000 down, owner will hold note." And, that was pretty much all it said. A quick call to the realtor made it fairly clear nothing was negotiable. We asked where it was, set up an appointment for that afternoon, went, saw and signed a binder for the asking price as-is, wrote a check, and closed in about two weeks. There was literally zero negotiation. The rate the sellers wanted and the term which they wanted were fine when compared to the value of the property. It was perfect.

The sellers were a retired couple looking to travel the country in a newly purchased motor home. The mortgage payment was calculated to pay for their gas and site fees. We made these payments to their attorney who made deposits into an account the sellers accessed as needed wherever they were. They were a lovely older couple living the dream and we helped them do just that. For our trouble we upgraded the bathroom and rented the house out for three years after which we sold it for $87,000 making $37,000 return on our $12,000 investment ($2k for the bath upgrade). During the three years we made a small positive cash flow and a healthy annual tax write-off but, a $37k return on a $12k investment is something a lot of people would like to see.

During the negotiation process for this home, everything was on the table and out in the open. Several other offers had come in and all were rejected out of hand. The owners were clear about what they wanted and they did their homework devising a deal that would work for both themselves as well as the buyer. They were honest and open and although we only stayed in touch through their attorney, I sincerely hope they lived a good long life and enjoyed their opportunity to see this great country.

# Part IV

# ENTREPRENEURIAL ASPECTS

Desire and experience are the bedmates of greed and overconfidence. Developing a dependable plan is essential to creating a lucrative real estate portfolio. Following that plan is imperative to its continued success. The attitude that gets you here is no different than the attitude that will be required to keep you here.

CHAPTER FOURTEEN

# Entrepreneurial Aspects of Income Property

That tenants represent more than income is a serious understatement. They are your customers. After all, without them you are but a land owner in this endeavor … a landowner with a lot of bills to pay out of your own pocket! You are in this to make money. Without tenants you can't do that. The goose that lays the golden egg is not the building you bought, it is the tenant to whom you have rented it. Care and feeding of the goose is manifest through your attention to the building you bought, but if you had purchased a self-storage complex, lawn care business, or a restaurant nothing would be different. Your job is to tend to the needs of your tenants, customers, patrons, or clients. Don't do it and they won't be yours for long. This is your job, and it is absolutely amazing how many people get it wrong.

The single common denominator in every business is the same: increase the bottom line. This is done by increasing income, decreasing costs, decreasing (and ultimately eliminating) debt. Rental property it is the exactly the same. The only part of owning a building that adds actual credible value (until the building is either sold or refinanced) is the return on investment. The combination of maximizing income and minimizing expense and debt leads directly to the correlation of the property value. To be truly successful, you have to do it all.

The single common denominator in every business is the same: increase the bottom line.

Rental Property Business Model

| KP - Key Partners | KA - Key Activities | VP - Value Proposition | CR - Customer Relationships | CS - Customer Segments |
|---|---|---|---|---|
| Bank<br>Insurance agent<br>Attorney<br>Accountant<br>Contractors<br>All other hired professionals | Provide living space<br>Maintain living space<br>Problem solving<br>Bookkeeping<br>Analysis and trending | Provide stable environment<br>Provide timely & quality services<br>Low cost operations<br>Imbue operational sense of pride | Humane understanding<br>Stable execution of expectations<br>Problem solving<br>Tact and diplomacy | Happy tenants<br>Minimal complaints |
| | KR - Key Recourses | | CH - Channels | |
| | Personal abilities<br>Personal knowledge<br>Maintenance crews | | Rapid responses<br>Consistent operations<br>Care & timeliness in activities<br>Neat, clean friendly environment<br>Listening and responding | |

| C$ - Cost Structure | R$ - Revenue Streams |
|---|---|
| Initial investments (down payment & closing costs)<br>Monthly operating expenses<br>Debt service<br>Replacement accounts | Rental income<br>Other income<br>Interest income from replacement, reserve and operating accounts<br>Fees and non-recurring charges |

Illustration 14.1—Rental Property Business Model

Many of the necessary day-to-day required tasks do not directly add to either the income stream or reduce the outlays and are therefore considered to be non-value added. But they are still tasks you must do to ensure the continued receipt of the rent checks. They themselves though, do not provide income. If you hire someone (*Key Partner*) to mow your lawn (*Value Proposition*), it is going to cost you money (*Cost Structure*). If you do it yourself (*Key Resource*), you will pay upfront costs for the mower, trimmer, and an ongoing expense for gas and oil (*Cost Structure*), but in neither case will the task itself generate income (*Revenue Stream*). Your choice in handling this minor task one way or the other may lessen the money you have to pay (*Cost Structure*), but it will not directly generate income (*Revenue Stream*). This then, by definition, becomes a non-value added task. The tenants will of course not see it in such light but you must. The tenants will see the end product, a neat and clean property (*Value Proposition*) and think nothing more of it. You will rarely receive a compliment on the way it all looks, but don't cut it for a month and their level of apparent disconnect will disappear rapidly (*Customer Segment*) which can have a negative effect on the income (*Revenue Stream*) should the tenants leave.

To maintain the proper outlook for the investment, this simple task must be divided into two parts. On the Business Model, simply divide the entire chart in half down the middle vertically. The left side is efficiency and the right side represents value. On the one hand is to get the lawn cut, trimmed, debris and trash picked up, and keep the place as neat as possible for the purpose of imbuing a degree of pride of residence for the tenants. On the other hand, it is to ensure the best value is generated for the method, time and money expended in the completion of the task. One perspective will keep the tenants happy, the other will maximize the value, your income level and the potential for future investments. This is a distinct difference and should be clearly understood.

This is true with every other aspect of the ownership as well. The heat is expected to work, the tenants are expected to be able to get out of the driveway after a snowfall, the roof is not supposed to leak etc. When you take care of these things it is always non-value added. It is simply the necessary upkeep to ensure those coveted rent checks continue to flow inward uninterrupted. **How you do these tasks affects the bottom line**. Balance between necessity and methodology cannot be ignored as it is essentially the definition of management. We all know if we ignore a leak it will not fix itself and go away. Delaying these repairs always has negative consequences. It will eventually cost more to repair, you will have damaged your credibility and good standing and so on.

Bookkeeping programs help you with all aspects of receivables, expenses, reports, P&L statements, tax forms etc, but they are no help in determining the validity of upgrades or analyzing options to returns for various improvements to be made.

My wife handles all the bookkeeping, check writing, bill paying, etc. for the properties we own. I collect and record the rents, late fees, water bill reimbursements from the tenants. I also monitor the income and all of the bills that come in against the properties. I analyze and set the rents according to areas averages and study the expenses to see trends and make changes. The way I do this is with the same spreadsheet we studied in chapters 10 and 12. I maintain these very same spreadsheets continuously updating them for every property. I also use the same to record replacement items dates, model and serial numbers and accurate mortgage balance and depreciation values. I will also compare property to property expenses, ratios and trends to see where improvements can be made. There are multiple reasons for doing this.

A property held for ten years might be a candidate for refinance, for a sale, or for an exchange. With the right zoning a large unused yard might be suited for a three-bay garage generating additional income, a coin-operated laundry can add huge convenience to the tenants allowing both an increase in income on the "other income" line as well as allow higher rents for an amenity. This is the side of the business where insight and foresight comes into play. It is the side for entrepreneurial spirit and in this capacity you need to analyze the entire problem before you take action on what you only perceive the problem as being. You need to get to the root cause and in your analysis, you need to make sure you are not creating a much bigger problem in the solution you have selected. My wife uses QuickBooks™ and handles the mechanical process of paying bills and making deposits (*Key Activities*) for preparation of taxes, P&L's (Profit and Loss) statements for banking and such. My spreadsheets are designed in Microsoft™ Excel and allow tending and analysis for cost reduction (*Value Proposition*).

# W H Y ?

In Chapter 12 we discussed a perceived problem with heating bills, but we only looked at it from one perspective—through our eyes during the vetting process of purchasing the building. But this issue had already been addressed once before. There was an entire analysis, capital expenditure and solution implemented previously, but with a dramatically different result. When the original heating plant failed, it became a problem the seller of this building needed to address.

In researching the problem he simply decided he no longer wished to pay some $4,000 a year in heating costs for this building (*Cost Structure*). He was forced to replace a huge old inefficient boiler and he sought an inexpensive way to do it. Having four separate hot water boilers would have been expensive as all the apartments were essentially tied in together. It would require opening all of the apartments at the same time, replacing all the radiators in each apartment and this would have to happen during the heating season. Remember, heating systems don't fail in summer. Electric heat is relatively inexpensive to install but he had old hot water radiators in the way of the electric baseboard units, so he went with radiant heat in the ceilings and was able to get it done quickly. The tenants' lives were disrupted but more importantly he was out from under a huge annual heating burden. In this case he either did not have the ability to analyze for himself (or the intelligence to ask for outside opinions) as to what options might be available. He shopped for price but did not consider the tenant's perspective (*Customer Segment*) in the equation. In the end he solved his problem but failed to create a win-win (*Channels*) with the tenants. Failing to secure a win-win becomes a loss. The result of this solution directly cost him $22,680 (*Revenue Stream*) in annual income which can be directly translated into an ultimate loss to this seller in excess of $100,000 in value added (*Cost Structure*).

He was successful in the elimination of the financial burden (*Positive Action*) of having to pay the heating bill for the building. He attempted to add value through decreased operating expenses, but he failed to recognize the cost was directly and profoundly impacting his income line (*Negative Action*) making a net zero gain. This is where I came in with the professionals, minimized the cost of the replacements (*Cost Structure*) and gave the tenants central air conditioning (*Value Proposition*) as a perk. This action did not alter the total monthly expense the tenants were paying however it substantially redirected where this money would go. Thus, from a tenants (*Cost Structure*) perspective nothing changed, it changed everything in their (*Value Proposition*) with air conditioning and in the (*Customer Segment*) in the removal of their monthly anxiety as they opened their electric bills. We made the right decisions from both sides of the equation and the increase in rent covered the cost entirely of these new heating systems in a single year. From our perspective, the (*Revenue Stream*) increase was huge.

You need the ability to take into consideration both sides of the equation. This is paramount to your being able to maximize your overall return, increase your property values, and to allow more choices. Here's the concept in simpler terms:

212 | The Reluctant Landlord's Guide

Consider fifth grade mathematics. Multiplying any positive number by any negative number will always generate a negative result. Multiplying two positive numbers will always result in a positive. Figure positive as "win" and negative as "lose." Win-win is the result of balancing the sides. The Business Model will help you do that. Now don't go getting all philosophical on me about two negatives always resulting in a positive. We are talking about investments and increasing costs and reducing revenue should not be what you are setting out to accomplish.

# FINANCIAL DISCIPLINE

The notion of landlords being business-minded entrepreneurs can be best described as being balance minded and financially disciplined. Financial discipline is most notably manifest in the creation and proper use of a replacement account.

A couple of really interesting things happen when you discipline yourself into using a replacement account. First and foremost, you will never find yourself putting major replacement items on your credit cards. You will most likely be replacing these items at the very time your income is reduced due to a vacancy. You won't find it easy to fill the vacancy with the place looking old and tattered, and if you try you will not rent at a premium. None of these things are good, but you can turn it all around. A tenant who moves out of a unit after occupying it for only 3 years and has destroyed the carpeting during that short stay should find themselves making up the difference for that carpet when you replace it. You can also add the lost income as an expense to them for down time while the apartment was not available waiting for the carpet to be installed. This comes out of the security deposit paid if they fail to take care of the place. When you have the exact life expectancy of the carpeting and the signed lease stipulating who is responsible for damages, it makes for a compelling story before a judge and generally will not be argued. In fact I have yet to be summoned before a judge to explain why a security deposit was not either fully or partially returned. However, if I am planning to hold some or all of a security deposit, I keep detailed accounting of the things I find during the walk-through including photographs. I will send the report to the tenant along with the photos and a check for the balance if any.

That's the bad side. On the good side is another host of things. I strive for long-term stable tenants. These tenants tend to remain as long as you take care of the place. If they move in when the appliances are all 5 years old and they keep the place clean and take care of things, as most tenants do, the life cycles will easily exceed your projections. I once had a tenant inform me he was taking a short vacation and the place would be empty for a week and would I please keep an eye on it. There had been a sale on a refrigerator several months earlier and I had taken advantage of and placed it in storage simply because it was too good a deal to pass up. I bought it in the event of a failure. I had picked this one up for only $313 and it was larger than the one he had. I asked if he would mind if I replaced it while he was away and he said fine. I replaced his 15 year old unit which was still operating and for which I was still depositing $5.95 every month into my replacement account. Since it was still running, I sold it for $50.00. The overall picture looked as such: the accounting line was reduced by the $1,126.39 which accumulated for this unit over its life, I added $50.00 for the sale of the old unit and the replacement cost $313.00. The total difference of $863.39 was mine to do with as I desired. The very next month $5.95 was deposited beginning the process anew.

Your replacement account should be funded at 100%. In an investment account that produces say 4% you will either not have to put the entire amount in or can enjoy the dividends paid as added income. The value of the account will change each month and if you make the necessary payments each month you only have checks coming out for your personal use and should never have to put any of your personal funds into the account. Having this account looks great in the eyes of the bank when you apply for the mortgage on your next property as well.

In addition to this you should also maintain 3 months' worth of total building expenses including, mortgage, taxes, insurance, utilities and all other anticipated expenses. Doing this gives you options most investing in real estate do not ever see and no one investing in anything other than real estate can possibly enjoy. I stepped out of sequence here to examine the importance of discipline and here is why.

# MAXIMIZING INCOME AND MINIMIZING EXPENSES

For this part of the conversation we need to recall the brief discussion in chapter 4 where we talked about the pyramid concept used by the banking industry. We also discussed the mental acuity towards being able to maximize income and minimize expenses in order to increase value. It is this increased value we need to examine and the options with which we have to put this to good use.

There are two terms we have used throughout the book: Return on Investment (ROI) and the Return on Equity (ROE). Return on Investment is used to determine validity of a purchase, whereas Return on Equity is only used after a purchase has been made and is used for growing an empire. The ROE is a relationship between the net-income the property produces divided by the equity in the property, and is the cornerstone of your financial pyramid's foundation. We use this relationship to determine the "highest and best use" for that equity for investment purposes.

For example: Let's say we bought a two-family property for $100k three years ago and through good curatorship, that building is worth $150k today. We will further assume we bought it with a conventional $80k mortgage at 5% which has been reduced by normal payments to $76,274.77. We therefore have an LTV (Loan-to-Value ratio) of 51% (77/150) and we would therefore "appear" to have accumulated close to $74k equity. If we earn a net income from this property of $2,500 we might think we have a return on that equity of only 3.4% ($2,500 / $74,000). But this is not entirely accurate. If we were to sell the property for the $150k we would be highly disappointed upon leaving that closing table.

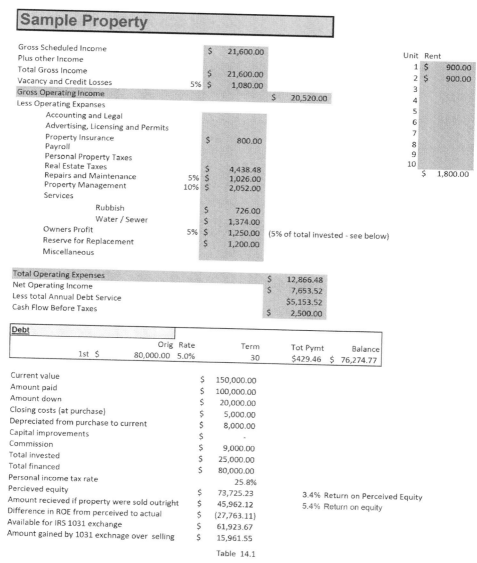

## Sample Property

| | | | |
|---|---|---|---|
| Gross Scheduled Income | | $ 21,600.00 | |
| Plus other Income | | | |
| Total Gross Income | | $ 21,600.00 | |
| Vacancy and Credit Losses | 5% | $ 1,080.00 | |
| Gross Operating Income | | | $ 20,520.00 |
| Less Operating Expanses | | | |
|     Accounting and Legal | | | |
|     Advertising, Licensing and Permits | | | |
|     Property Insurance | | $ 800.00 | |
|     Payroll | | | |
|     Personal Property Taxes | | | |
|     Real Estate Taxes | | $ 4,438.48 | |
|     Repairs and Maintenance | 5% | $ 1,026.00 | |
|     Property Management | 10% | $ 2,052.00 | |
|     Services | | | |
|         Rubbish | | $ 726.00 | |
|         Water / Sewer | | $ 1,374.00 | |
|     Owners Profit | 5% | $ 1,250.00 | (5% of total invested - see below) |
|     Reserve for Replacement | | $ 1,200.00 | |
|     Miscellaneous | | | |
| Total Operating Expenses | | $ 12,866.48 | |
| Net Operating Income | | $ 7,653.52 | |
| Less total Annual Debt Service | | $5,153.52 | |
| Cash Flow Before Taxes | | $ 2,500.00 | |

| Unit | Rent | |
|---|---|---|
| 1 | $ | 900.00 |
| 2 | $ | 900.00 |
| 3 | | |
| 4 | | |
| 5 | | |
| 6 | | |
| 7 | | |
| 8 | | |
| 9 | | |
| 10 | | |
| | $ | 1,800.00 |

### Debt

| | Orig | Rate | Term | Tot Pymt | Balance |
|---|---|---|---|---|---|
| 1st $ | 80,000.00 | 5.0% | 30 | $429.46 | $ 76,274.77 |

| | | |
|---|---|---|
| Current value | $ 150,000.00 | |
| Amount paid | $ 100,000.00 | |
| Amount down | $ 20,000.00 | |
| Closing costs (at purchase) | $ 5,000.00 | |
| Depreciated from purchase to current | $ 8,000.00 | |
| Capital improvements | $ - | |
| Commission | $ 9,000.00 | |
| Total invested | $ 25,000.00 | |
| Total financed | $ 80,000.00 | |
| Personal income tax rate | 25.8% | |
| Percieved equity | $ 73,725.23 | 3.4% Return on Perceived Equity |
| Amount recieved if property were sold outright | $ 45,962.12 | 5.4% Return on equity |
| Difference in ROE from perceived to actual | $ (27,763.11) | |
| Available for IRS 1031 exchange | $ 61,923.67 | |
| Amount gained by 1031 exchnage over selling | $ 15,961.55 | |

Table 14.1

## Table 14.2—Sample Property

Think back to chapter 3 where we did the comparisons. In this case there are things we need to remember. First, I would never sell a piece of real estate without the professional assistance of a broker. That will run 6% of the selling price or $9k. Then there is the tax issue to deal with. We have been taking depreciation on the property for 3 years and as such we have depreciated the property by $8,000 some of which will rightfully go back to Uncle Sam. You would be left with a check for about $63,000, *but* you would be paying 25.8% in taxes. We left you in the federal 15% bracket but, add a health care tax of 3.8% and a state (NY in my case) of 7% and you would walk away with an after tax check for only about $46,000. Quite a difference from the $74,000 you focused on.

If I were to look only at the value of the building vs. the balance of the loan I could easily come to the conclusion that at 3.4% ROE, I could do better in the stock market and I might be tempted to do so. But it is not a 3.4% return, it is a 5.4% return. It is not equity of $74k it is only $46k, ($2,500 / $46,000) and that might make it a little more enticing to stay in the game. And yet, this is actually where the game begins. Selling this property and buying another would only get you a building worth little more than this one already is. If $40k is the available 20% down payment (assume $6k for closing costs) then $40 /.20 = $200k and you will have another tenant / landlord vetting process all over again.

Don't be disappointed by this, but do understand it. If this scenario were real you would have received over 3 years, income of $7,500, tax write-offs worth $2,600 (federal and state tax saved on the depreciated amounts) and of course that check for $46,000. This all adds up to a total of $56,100. Your investment cost you $25,000 in down payment and closing costs and doubling your money in less than 3 years is better than any of the scenarios outlined in chapter 3. Not a bad thing. But you can do better. Much better.

# BUILDING YOUR PORTFOLIO

This is the point where it becomes necessary to become the true entrepreneur as we outlined in the beginning of this chapter. You have to use the good curatorship to achieve the properties' potential value. Once this is done though, there is a way to avoid all of the taxes except the healthcare 3.8%. A way that essentially allows you to use all of the after cost equity, in this case of $62,000 and that is through a formal IRS Code Section 1031 Real Estate Exchange. This allows you to roll the entire equity (less the commission, closing costs and healthcare tax) into a new (generally larger and more valued) property of "like kind." It has to be real estate, and cannot be stocks or bonds. In our example you would have received that same check for $62,000 but instead of paying 25.8% to Uncle Sam, you would have used it without paying any tax (except the 3.8% healthcare tax) by using it as the down payment for a 4-family property worth $300k. This is an extremely powerful tool when used properly.

If you do this, the original investment of $20k (plus $5k closing costs) on the original $100k 2-family building now represents the entire down payment, and a good portion of the closing costs on a 4-family income property worth nearly a third of a million dollars. In a very short period of time it is possible to be generating a net income per year that exceeds the total initial investment you made when buying the original 2-family property.

This process is not synonymous with "flipping" properties. You should use the same analysis and business approach. Once you have a solid income producing property in your portfolio, maintain it, and enjoy the benefits.

Things to be considered when using these tools to build your portfolio of properties: goals, foundations, and reserve and replacement accounts. A 4-family income property will need a bigger reserve—don't forget this. If you garnered the discipline and banked the annual income you have the reserve and will do fine, if not, you are simply not ready. Markets are often too fickle for these exchanges to take place. A buyer's market will get you out of the building you currently own, but may cost you too much to get your next property. A seller's market will present choice properties all over the place, but without buyers for yours. Reading the tea leaves is crucial, but even this can be manipulated if you possess the right knowledge.

In the first chapter I described the client who was developing the golf course as an industrial park. If you should find yourself in a stagnant market when you stumble across a deal simply too good to pass up but cannot find a buyer for the property you have earmarked for the exchange, offering an "Option" (legally binding instrument of intent for a purchase at a set price and by some future date and with an expiration attached) on the new property you desire may indeed be the win-win for both buyer and seller you need. It will give the seller a cash incentive to hold the property for whatever timeframe you agree to, and will give you time to market and sell your original property. This is the reason I put so much emphasis in chapters 2 - 5 on the power and necessity of expanding your knowledge base. In this case, knowledge is paramount to success. Books on options are as just as plentiful and available as 1031 exchanges. Do not ever attempt to do any 1031 exchange without a very good attorney and an accountant. If the paperwork is not perfect you may be liable for the tax you just used to buy another property.

It takes time to prepare your property as well as ratchet-up your fiscal discipline to be able to take advantage of these opportunities. A 4-family property replacement account will likely be about twice that of a 2-family account, but if you have properly set up your accounts you will instantly have one half of the 4-family account necessary. When you roll over your old fully funded account you may actually have much more than half if you have allowed the **bold** lines to grow unmolested. Never does everything in a building fail at the same time, and starting out with an account half funded is a great place to start. I very seriously recommend that both your 3-month expense account and your replacement accounts be once again funded to 100% before you look to trade up again, in this next case—to your first eight-unit complex.

Be careful or greed and overconfidence can start to take control. There have been too many to mention failed millionaire real estate investors down this road. You are human, you do not have a Teflon suit and you cannot fly. So, be smart instead!

When your financial house is in order, read all you can on exchanges and options and most importantly, surround yourself with the best professionals you can find. They are worth their weight in gold.

Refinancing is another option indicated when analyzing the ROI and ROE on properties but I caution you against taking cash out of the equity position unless you have a very sound and specific investment use for that money. A new car is not a good use.

I will not consider refinancing a property when the cost of doing so will not be returned in less than two years. In other words the reduction in my payments will have to be < 1/24 of the cost to me of the transaction. If I know I can save $200 a month on the debt service payments then the transaction will have to be able to be concluded for < $4,800 (24 x $200). This is very easy to do when rates are declining and can be extremely difficult when rates are rising.

As a rule I don't like to spend money on closing costs. It has to be very cost effective to entice me to do this, but it does happen. If I have a property LTV drop to the 40% range, but am not able to recover the closing costs in less than 24 months I will seek peace with my inner self and be patient. I waited three years to refinance that 4-family property, got the rate to 4% flat and recovered the costs in 22.9 months.

I try to only use equity removed from properties to purchase other properties or perhaps make improvements to existing properties if it will raise the income (*Revenue Stream*) and or decrease the costs (*Cost Structure*) and thereby increase the property value accordingly. None of these things are possible with any investment other than real estate. It might be compared to owning a stock that splits but you have no control over these things.

In the realm of 1031 exchanges it will always be in your interest to undersell an existing property instead of overbuying a new property. Sell for less if necessary, but don't pay more than any property is worth, and don't buy a bigger property than the equity will comfortably support. If you have a property in mind you want to sell and think it will generate $100k in equity don't look for a $600k building to buy. Settle for that nice $400k building. If you only net $80k you are still in the clear and will not have problems with banks on the new property or worse, with cash flow by overextending.

Take baby steps. Dave Ramsey named his course aptly. It takes time. Donald Trump can do whatever he likes. You are not there yet.

CHAPTER FIFTEEN

# Markets

In October of 1978 the prime rate rose above 10% for the second time in modern history. The first time it went over 10% was in the early 70s. It reached a staggering height of 20% in December of 1980 and did not drop back below 10% until June of 1985. That's a total of eight years at over 10% prime rate. Mortgage rates are generally a couple of points above prime. It was during this time that Robert Allen, Albert Lowery, Bill Nickerson, and numerous other real estate gurus made names for themselves. This was also the time frame I first stuck a toe into the real estate market. The market at the time could be described as less than perfect, but property did not stop changing hands and profits were made all around. People found ways to profit even with mortgage rates over 20%. The worst single day stock market drop was not in 1929 but in 1987. The current "Real Estate Bust" began in 2008 and continues persistently hemorrhaging throughout financial markets even today. We will take a quick look at this latest issue since most readers are still able to relate and while little has yet to be clouded by manufactured histories and conspiracy theorists.

In 1938 the U.S. Government created the Federal National Mortgage Association (Fannie Mae) to purchase, bundle, and sell home mortgages to investors as bond instruments (see chapter 4). This was created essentially to extend the term of the loans banks could issue to home buyers from 3 to 5 years to 20 and even 30 years. This was a direct response to the high amount of foreclosures during the 1929 market crash when mortgages were short term instruments. The value of home prices during the depression only dropped by 25% but a higher percentage of homeowners became homeless due to the short term mortgages being refinanced at higher rates which the homeowners simply could not pay.[1] In 1970 the government also created a competitor for Fannie Mae establishing the Federal Home Loan Mortgage Corporation (Freddie Mac).

During the Carter Administration when interest rates rose to over 20% banks with these long term instruments were found to holding the short end of the stick and losing money daily on the long term low interest rates they had in their portfolios. The cost of borrowing funds to lend was costing more than the interest received on the old loans on the books and their answer was the adjustable rate mortgage. Banks would be safe now no matter what the market did. Not so much the homeowner. All went well for many years until it was determined again by government that the banks that were originating all those mortgages were not doing so evenly across racial, ethnic, and minority lines.

In 1994 a strong push was initiated to begin increasing home ownership across these lines with "The National Homeownership Strategy: Partners in the American Dream."[2]

From this it was established that Freddie and Fannie were to begin taking greater risks to ensure more minority home loans were accepted into the packages bundled by Freddie and Fannie to the investors who bought these government backed securities. The notion behind this action was the expansion of pride of home ownership across these racial, ethnic, and minority lines. This was the noble yet gregarious desire behind this strategy.[3] However, as the saying goes, life gets in the way of plans, or as I like to say, "Make sure the fix doesn't cause a bigger problem." Between adjustable rate mortgages and an across the board reduction in qualification criteria lies a recipe for disaster which no-one saw coming.

In essence this arrangement meant that lenders (banks writing the original mortgages) could really not turn people away from the housing market even if their credit and track record indicated they should have been. The banks were mandated by Congress to reduce the standards on which they would write loans and Fannie Mae and Freddy Mac were mandated to continue buying these mortgages. Investors buying them would still have high grade investments backed by the full faith and trust of the United States Government. Real estate agents were guaranteed buyers would qualify, mortgage originators were guaranteed commissions, banks were guaranteed their mortgages would be accepted and investors were guaranteed a return on their investment. We were all living in a perfect world.

We, however, do not live in a perfect world.

On 15 September, 2008, Merrill Lynch sold itself to Bank of America, Lehman Brothers filed for bankruptcy, and the Dow Jones lost 504 points. In the next 18 months fully half of the value of Wall Street had evaporated, unemployment would rise from 6.1 to over 10% and the Federal government would bail out or outright purchase $204,808,576,320[4] worth of banks and financial institutions. With half of Wall Street valuation gone—corporate, state and educational retirement plans found themselves severely short of mandated funding levels, taxes rose; cuts to services were made, deficits grew ... I am sure by now you get the idea.

Five years later, the dust had far from settled, but enough study on the sub-prime market has been accomplished for subjective conclusions to be made thus; the Congress blamed the investors, investors blame Freddie and Fannie, Freddie and Fannie blamed the banks, the banks blamed the originators, the originators blamed the buyers, and the buyers are in foreclosure.

It will all work out though, Congress is looking into fixing the foreclosure problem.

In early to mid-2000s anyone could buy a home because no one was turned away from getting a mortgage. Why? Because government mandated homeownership and these mortgage notes had investors with cash lined up around the globe to buy them because they were guaranteed by the full faith and trust of the U.S. Government … *and* the bonds paid high returns. U.S. Saving bonds are backed by the U.S. Government and today pay a paltry 0.75%. Mortgage backed securities were paying 6% and more with essentially the same guarantees. Which would you buy?

# N E W   E R A

Things are a bit different today. The Freddie Mac and Fannie Mae (of 1994) have died.

Everyone looks for an edge. The world of finance is the most prevalent. Whatever Congress and the Senate conjure as well abiding notions for the populace will be met with two things: opportunists on the demand side and on the supply side, there will be opportunists. But usually more than just one supply/demand courtship will emerge.

Revisiting the landscape between 1994 and 2008 we see the following picture. Retrospectively only of course. In housing, demand side opportunists used the plan to purchase the home they wanted, taking advantage of these new laws. On the supply side, people sold their homes for higher prices due to this greater demand and moved up to larger homes themselves.

In financing, demand side opportunists hired mortgage origination officers and underwriters. On the supply side bankers and mortgage brokers looked to Wall Street for ways to move the vast increases in mortgages they wrote quickly in order to perpetuate the movement in higher demand.

In marketing, demand mandated bundling of mortgage securities to larger investors, pension plans and the like. Supply side required Wall Street to invent unique marketing campaigns for expanding the pool of required cash, called them derivatives and built an entire new industry.

Investors on the demand side were eager to take advantage of this new market and began betting on the futures, the supply side took loans against the securities to expand and perpetuate the appetite ... and so on and so on. This is how a bubble is built, too many opportunists getting together. Each with their own little niche and plans to make it big. Take away any one piece and the whole thing comes crashing down.

On September 15, 2008 the piece was taken away. Although it had been brewing for some time, it made a formal appearance in the supply side of the investors' pool under the name of Lehman Brothers. In the end, the total combined losses perpetrated by the housing bubble exceed 8 trillion dollars. Those with fortitude, foresight, and with a long term plan were not directly affected. I personally had two of my children attending a private university during this entire time frame and neither they nor I was affected.

Hundreds of thousands of people lost their shirts as well as their homes when the bubble burst in 2008. Take away any one of the factors and the bubble stops growing, but so long as everyone is making money, and rest assured it really is about the money, nobody ever cares until it is too late. Congress was only trying to help "the little guy" by making housing affordable. They couldn't mandate the price so they relaxed the requirements. Are the realtors really going to be expected not to show buyers a home they want to buy? No, someone else will simply get the commission. Can bankers and mortgage brokers be expected to turn prospective buyers away, they couldn't even if they wanted to lest they be sued for discrimination. Could Wall Street be expected to say sorry, we don't want several billion dollars in commissions selling your securities. Would you? Every snowflake in an avalanche claims innocent. Yet all point fingers on the morning after.

The issue here is these things happen. They happen frequently. And they are not going to stop because although we have learned the lesson, we are—each and every one of us—an opportunist. And if an opportunity presents itself, we will take it.

How you fared in this upheaval was entirely dependent on what you were doing during this time. If you were an opportunist taking advantage of rapidly rising housing prices by flipping properties then you had better have read the tea leaves real well. Most did not. Perhaps you were one of the many that traded up, or bought with nothing down and went underwater. But, if you are of the Warren Buffet mindset, buying for the long haul, then this major market meltdown was a minor inconvenience, some other investors' problems and not so much your own.

In my particular situation I wrote down over half a million in value but never climbed above 64% encumbered loan to value ratio. This is important. Are you going to strive to buy the planet or do you have realistic and down to earth goals? Real estate is unique but you have to look at it in those unique terms. I wrote down $500,000 in value, but did not lose one dime. Lehman failed because it got greedy and increased its assets to equity from 24:1 to 31:1. This, from the perspective we have been using was reducing their equity

> **Will you strive to buy the planet or have realistic goals?**

position from 5% to 3%. Sure they made a lot more than I ever will but remember back to chapter 3 where we discussed how if you are going to collapse, the big and little still fall at the same rate. If you properly prepare your outlook then this becomes a trip you need not take. If you do though, you will both take the same time to arrive at rock bottom.

The larger ones make bigger stains on the sidewalk when they land.

So, what did I lose? Nothing. Time has a nice little tendency to heal all wounds in real estate, as long as the initial loss does not push you over the brink into insolvency. Unfortunately, this is exactly what happened to tens of thousands of folks between 2008 and 2011. I bought two properties in 2007. As I mentioned in chapter 12, one of those was a disastrous 4-family property which I turned into a polished gem of an asset and by 2012, refinanced it realizing a net increase in equity during the worst market of my career.

You have complete control of your actions. You have no control over the markets. It does not matter one iota what the market is doing. It only matters what you are doing in that market.

This market will settle down. Prices will stabilize. People will tire of paying rent and the housing market will once again fall comfortably into equilibrium. This is still America. It is still the strongest. It is still the land of the free and home of the brave. It remains the most innovative country on this planet. Why? Because we allow new markets to try and fail. And when they fail, we fix them and move on. It tends to be these fixes we put in place that historically generate the unintended consequences which give rise to the next generation of opportunity and the consequences thereof.

The ideas, at the time, are well received. On the heels of 1,000 bank failures in the 80s the opportunity was called the Adjustable Rate Mortgage. In the early 90s it was relaxing the credit requirements to put everyone in America in their own home. The levels of pride were supposed to climb, as would wealth. But people with no vested interest will never care as much as those who have a large stake in the enterprises in which they involve themselves.

# JUST WALK AWAY . . .

A good friend of mine was in the process of buying a new home for herself back about 1998. She owned a townhouse at the time and had built some equity and was moving up. The market was just beginning to weaken and sales were dropping on townhouses precipitously when she approached the bank to discuss the new mortgage. What she was told back then set the stage for things to come. The mortgage banker for the new home, a huge national name, told her "… all she would need is a fictitious lease drawn up for the townhouse showing enough income to cover the existing mortgage. Once you are in the new home, just walk away." Translation: walk away from the existing townhouse mortgage. "It's done all the time."

This was a bank telling a customer to walk away from her mortgage payments from a competing bank! Let the house go into foreclosure. So what? You'll get what you want. The rationale for this recommendation was the commission this new mortgage broker would receive had they completed the deal. The seeds were set for the 2008 market housing crash long before 2008 arrived.

A lot of potential buyers today have the wherewithal to purchase homes but cannot qualify for the loans under the new guidelines. This is increasing the demand for apartments.

The market will turn around. No question about it. The stock market is at 15,000, doubled from the 2009 lows. Few thought it would ever come back hiding behind clichés such as "This time is different," and "I missed it." I know one man in particular that rode his retirement account in the stock market all the way from 14,000 to 8,000 before he sold. Last I spoke to him he still had not gotten back in. But he will! Probably the day it breaks 20,000. Buy low, sell high, refers to everything. Unfortunately stamina and mental fortitude often force us into selling low and buying high. Yet the vast majority don't have this problem. They make no investments at all. I do not fear offending them, they have not read this far. For those who have, capitalize on opportunities. They abound before you.

As Wayne Gretzky would say, "You miss 100% of the shots you don't take." I leave you in poetry:

## Investors Remorse Poem

I hesitate to make a list
Of countless transactions I have missed.
Bonanzas that were in my grip—
I watched them through my fingers slip.
The windfalls which I should have bought
Were lost because I over thought.
I thought of this, I thought of that,
I could have sworn I smelled a rat,
And while I thought things over twice,
Another grabbed them at the price.
It seems I always hesitate,
Then make my mind up much too late.
A very cautious man am I
And that is why I never buy.

When developments rose on Oak and Third
The prices asked I felt absurd.
Whole block fronts—black with soot—
Were priced at thirty bucks a foot!

When I wouldn't even make a bid,
Others didn't lose a beat!
When Newport Beach was cheap barren land,
I could have had a heap of sand.
When Palm Springs was the place to buy,
I thought the climate was much to dry.
Invest in Orange County—that is the spot!
My sixth sense warned me I should not.
A very prudent man am I
And that is why I never buy.

When others culled sprawling farms
And welcomed deals with open arms—
A corner here, ten acres there,
Compounding values year by year,
I choose to think and as I thought,
They bought the deals I should have bought.
The golden chance I had then
Are lost and will not come again.
Today I cannot be enticed
For everything is so overpriced.
The deals of yesteryear are dead;
The market is soft—and so is my head.
Last night I had a fearful dream,
I know I wakened with a scream;
Some Indians approached my bed—
For trinkets on the barrelhead
In dollar bills worth twenty four

And nothing less and nothing more.
They would sell Manhattan Isle to me
The most I would go was twenty three.
The Indian scowled: "Not on a bet":
And sold to Peter Minuit.
At times a teardrop drowns my eye
For deals I had, but didn't buy.
And now life's saddest words I pen—
"If only I would invest NOW … and then!

—Anonymous

This poem was written by the pinnacle of insecurity. The truth is, most people do not invest. But it is not this inaction that causes me to label this author accordingly. The poem is quite good. However, the thing that jumped off the page to me was not profound diction or an outward ability to wax eloquent expressing confusion or an inability to recognize value, but that the author, so incredibly untrusting of his ability, not only failed to invest, he failed as a writer as well … he couldn't even muster enough bravado to scribe his own name.

Follow your own destiny down that path less traveled and let no man lead you astray.

Good luck. I'd love to hear of your success!

# www.pritchardconsultinginc.com

## Endnotes

1. https://docs.google.com/viewer?a=v&q=cache:JXznjz9WVIQJ:realesta te.wharton.upenn.edu/review/%3Fdownload%3D125+&hl=en&gl=us& pid=bl&srcid=ADGEESjM6EJXiDX5_84lxFSSMP3XMKLdzgV5xZbq_ mg86z_fTutk2Uf7Cw7yFF-6rwLi71IjSObFKIGLcJeHcOq30H6KweWEbP ciLuFI05mRGzBMP8Qizl6DtTDckH2jC-wIqimObvBP&sig=AHIEtbTYI-PbaE35l9LoHnxzKZeiCtewSw

2. http://www.businessweek.com/the_thread/hotproperty/archives/2008/02/ clintons_drive.html

3. http://www.bloomberg.com/news/2010-06-13/fannie-freddie-fix-expands-to-160-billion-with-worst-case-at-1-trillion.html

4. http://money.cnn.com/news/specials/storysupplement/bankbailout/

# APPENDIX

# Recommended Reading List

## PART 1

The problem with reading these kinds of books is that most people today are looking for an immediate answer to a specific question. It is an "instant gratification" society. Unfortunately there is too little value seen for this material in many youth, but for the person trying to develop an understanding and the ability to operate on a different level these are invaluable!

- *Financial Peace University* (9 week course) - Dave Ramsey, for those in need of financial stability.

- *The Truth About Money* – Ric Edelman, buy it, place it prominently, refer to it frequently.

- *The Lies About Money* – Ric Edleman, use the excess income after funding your replacement account to feed other investment accounts or use to create your real estate accounts.

- *The Little Book of Common Sense Investing* – John C. Bogle, easy to read, hard to apply.

- *The Clash of the Cultures* – John C. Bogle, mind boggling (no pun intended) and somewhat frightening inside look at the world of the mutual fund industry.

- *Stop Acting Rich* – Dr Thomas Stanley, this and the next two Stanley books are in my library. All three are great and should form the basis for your underlying approach to upgrading your financial habits.

- *The Millionaire Next Door* – Dr. Thomas Stanley

- *The Millionaire Mind* - Dr. Stanley Thomas

- *20 Retirement Decisions You Need to Make Right Now* – Ray E. Levitre, time is never the friend of financial procrastination. I bought my daughter this book when she was 20.

- *Rescue Your Money* – Ric Edleman, a short book with a strong message.

- *How to Set Goals* – Craig Ballantyne, there are thousands of goal orientated books, this is short and a great introductory lesson applicable across many fields of endeavor, and its principals are easy to engage.

- *Getting To Yes* – Roger Fisher and William Ury, good negotiating skills are great to have and are applicable to everything in life.

- *Snowball, Warren Buffet and the Business of Life* – Alice Schroeder

In addition, enjoy the psychological financial antithesis added for those readers who willingly place blind trust that others have your best interest at heart;

- *Greed and Glory on Wall Street* – Ken Auletta, the Fall of the House of Lehman

- *False Profits* – Peter Truell and Larry Gurwin

- *Chain of Blame* – Paul Muolo and Mathew Padilla, this is a good analysis of the afterglow of the changes to the laws enacted by congress which partially empowered the events leading up to the housing crisis. Never forget, every snowflake in an avalanche claims innocent.

- *Takeover, The New Wall Street Warriors, The Men, The Money, The Impact* – Moria Johnston. There are thousands more from this group as well. Enron, Madoff, pages 1 through 6 of the typical newspaper.

# PART 2

There are literally thousands of such titles and authors and are best read when the desire to fall off the goal track is strongest. Covey and Collins both have many books in print, read them all. A few additional authors: Napolean Hill, John Maxwell, Patrick Lencioni, and many more.

- *The 7 Habits of Highly Effective People* - Steven Covey

- *The Toyota Way to Leadership* – Jeffery K. Liker, Gary L. Convis, understand and utilize the principals and art of delegating authority while maintaining and accepting responsibility.

- *Level Five Leadership* – Jim Collins, I have given this book as a gift to people I felt were worthy. I use the same attitudes with employees as I do with tenants.

# PART 3

- *The Millionaire Real Estate Investor* – Gary Keller - one of the best on real estate investing and the only such book on the list.

# PART 4

I originally listed books about 1031 exchanges, but tax law changes require current views. If you find the need, ask a good real estate attorney and sit with your accountant.

   ✆ *Business Model Generation* - Alexander Osterwalder & Yves Pigneur. On the cover is the statement, "You're holding a handbook for visionaries..." but I found this too narrow. The concepts apply to Google and GE, but they also apply to income property, lawn care and dog walking if that's how you earn a living.

Knowing your credit score is important. Understanding what that score means is imperative. Here are som great credit report resources.

   ✆ *https://www.annualcreditreport.com/cra/index.jsp*

Use this site to see your credit report free of charge, see the web address for understanding what is on the report or, go to your desk copy of Ric Edleman's, *The Truth About Money* section on "Understanding your Credit Report." This site will not give you your credit score, just the reports that go into creating that score.

   ✆ *http://www.myfico.com/CreditEducation/articles/*

Clear and useful tips on understanding the information found on your credit report. Good education source for identifying underlying results of the financial actions you take.

40875349R00140

Made in the USA
Lexington, KY
21 April 2015